SPARK

Amith Prabhu is a pioneering Public Relations and reputation management professional with over twenty years of experience. He has worked in India and in the USA at leading marketing communication companies. He is the co-founder of India's only weekend offsite summit for the profession, PRAXIS. He serves on the international board of the Global Alliance (GA). He is the founding dean at the School of Communications & Reputation (SCoRe) in Mumbai. He has a postgraduate degree in Public Relations and communication management from Symbiosis Institute of Media and Communication. He lives in Gurgaon. He can be found on Twitter @amithpr.

Sarika Chavan is the founder of Sparkle Gift Cards and the director of social impact at The PRomise Foundation. She is a Public Relations professional with over nineteen years of work experience. Her last stint was at Weber Shandwick Mumbai, where she was vice president—client experience. Previously she was employed at Adfactors PR, Text100 (now known as Archetype) and Perfect Relations. She writes the longest-running monthly book review column. She has a postgraduate diploma from the Xavier Institute of Communications. She lives in Mumbai. She can be found on Twitter @sourikka.

EDITED BY
AMITH
PRABHU
AND
SARIKA
CHAVAN

SPARK

STORIES AND INSIGHTS FROM INDIA'S PUBLIC RELATIONS PIONEERS

Published by Westland Business, an imprint of Westland Books, a division of Nasadiya Technologies Private Limited, in 2024

No. 269/2B, First Floor, 'Irai Arul', Vimalraj Street, Nethaji Nagar, Alapakkam Main Road, Maduravoyal, Chennai 600095

ISBN: 9789360454395

10 9 8 7 6 5 4 3 2 1

Typeset by Mukul

Printed at Thomson Press (India) Ltd

We would like to dedicate this book to our parents, especially Sarika's father, the late Anil Salian and Amith's mother, the late Ethel Prabhu.

Contents

Foreword by Arun Sudhaman ix
Introduction xiii

1 Sunil Agarwal 1
2 Atul Ahluwalia 5
3 Madan Bahal 15
4 Manisha Chaudhary 29
5 Kunal Kishore Sinha 40
6 Dilip Cherian 52
7 Rajiv Desai 62
8 Sunil Gautam 71
9 Aman Gupta 78
10 Shivani Gupta 88
11 Vineet Handa 99
12 Archana Jain 107
13 Ashish Jalan 117

14 Zacharia James 126

15 Samir Kale 134

16 Bobby Kewalramani 143

17 Nikhil Khanna 151

18 Nandita Lakshmanan 155

19 Gaurav Patra 170

20 Roger C.B. Pereira 176

21 Bela Rajan 185

22 N. Sundar Rajan 195

23 Prema Sagar 205

24 Rishi Seth 216

Acknowledgements 223

Foreword

by Arun Sudhaman
CEO and Editor-in-Chief, PRovoke Media

INDIA'S EMERGENCE ON THE GLOBAL PUBLIC RELATIONS (PR) stage is no accident, but the logical progression of the innovation and momentum that continues to reflect the nation's essential diversity and dynamism. Increasingly, India's vibrant PR community is setting global trends rather than merely following them—shaping narratives, building relationships and, crucially, playing a leadership role beyond the country's borders.

Accordingly, it is with great pleasure and anticipation that I introduce this seminal work, which captures the essence of India's PR revolution through the voices of its most influential architects.

This book is more than a collection of stories—it is a testament to the transformative power of vision, perseverance and adaptability. The editors transcend individual success stories to paint an engrossing portrait, not just of a profession in flux, but of the leadership required to navigate a fast-changing environment of transformation.

The structure of each profile—life sketch, evolution of PR and future vision—offers an unforgettable, multi-dimensional view of these leaders. Through their personal journeys, we witness the birth and growth of India's PR consultancy landscape. These are not just business stories but human tales, filled with challenges overcome, opportunities seized and lessons learnt.

As we explore their perspectives on the evolution of PR, we better understand how India's PR firms are adapting to seismic shifts in technology, media consumption and stakeholder expectations. From the advent of digital platforms to the rise of content marketing and the increasing emphasis on data-driven strategies, these leaders have not just witnessed change—they have driven it.

Perhaps most compelling are their visions for the future. In a world where the lines between PR, marketing and digital communications continue to blur, these thought leaders offer their predictions and aspirations for where the profession is headed. Their forward-thinking approaches provide a roadmap for the next generation of PR professionals, not just in India but globally.

What makes this book even more significant is its timing. We stand on the cusp of further technological change, with artificial intelligence poised to reshape communications yet again. Which helps to explain why the wisdom contained in these pages is essential reading. The leaders featured here have already navigated multiple paradigm shifts; their insights on preparing for the next wave are invaluable.

As we look to the future, it's clear that the role of PR only becomes more critical. In a world grappling with issues of trust, authenticity and information overload, the ability to craft authentic narratives and foster genuine relationships is indispensable. The leaders profiled in this book demonstrate what it means to rise to this challenge.

To the aspiring PR professionals who will read this book: let these stories inspire you. To the veterans of the profession: let these visions challenge you to continue innovating. And to all readers: let this collection serve as a reminder of the power of effective communication to drive progress, transform societies and shape our world.

The PR business in India has come of age, and this book is both a celebration of that journey and a glimpse into an exciting future. I commend the authors for their vision in bringing these stories together, and I have no doubt that this work will become an essential reference for anyone interested in the past, present and future of Public Relations.

Introduction

THE IDEA FOR THIS BOOK GERMINATED FROM A SIMPLE thought—what if we could capture and document the stories of the pioneers who founded Public Relations (PR) firms in India during the early 1990s and 2000s? These are the trailblazers who not only built their firms from the ground up but also paved the way for countless others in the field. Their stories are rich with insights, lessons and experiences that PR professionals can learn from and be inspired by.

The 1990s marked a time of liberalisation of the economy in India, and it was during this period that many PR firms emerged. The stories captured in this book take you back to those early days, a time when the way we live and work today was almost unimaginable. Things we now take for granted—like enjoying a burger or wearing trendy jeans—were just starting to make their way into the Indian market. It's hard for today's generation to fathom a time when press releases were handwritten or typed on a typewriter and delivered in person, but that's exactly what many of these founders had to do with no internet and email. It was an era where even mobile phones weren't commonplace.

These founders didn't just create businesses—they laid the foundations for the employment journeys of many who would go on to shape the future of the profession. Some even launched their own firms after learning from these inspiring leaders.

One of the key takeaways that resonates with us is the enduring power of relationships. The strong bonds these PR pioneers forged with their clients were the foundation of their success, with many still serving the very clients they first brought on board—something rare in today's fast-paced, short-term world. Another prominent theme in these stories is the importance of being resilient. Whether it was launching campaigns or handling crises, creativity and innovation were the cornerstones that helped sustain these long-standing relationships, nurturing and safeguarding the reputations of numerous brands over the years.

Bringing this idea to life was not an easy journey. We began in May 2024, conceptualising this project with a clear goal in mind, but transforming that vision into reality required time, dedication and the willingness of these incredible individuals to share their stories despite their busy schedules. From conducting interviews to transcribing and piecing together each narrative, it has been a labour of love.

We were fortunate that Westland accepted our proposal for this book. And the outcome of these efforts is here for you to see. We hope you get inspired in the same way we were, by listening to and reading these fascinating stories. Each life sketch has the potential to become a mini biopic.

Every story in this book is a testament to the power of creativity and the indomitable spirit of these founders. Within these pages, readers will discover not only personal journeys but also campaigns and moments that will resonate deeply. We chose to present these stories in alphabetical order by last name, as each one holds equal importance, and no one story can outshine another. (We have kept profiles of individuals back to back in cases where they are life partners.)

Each chapter is divided into three parts. The first part, which is our personal favourite, delves into the founder's early life and professional journey, offering a glimpse into the experiences that shaped their success. The second part reflects on how they have witnessed the PR profession evolve over the years, providing invaluable insights into the transformation of the practice. The third part focuses on their views about the future of PR, sharing their predictions and advice for what lies ahead. These perspectives are a must-read for any aspiring PR professional looking to become an effective leader and wanting to learn from the best. This is also a must-read for anyone who is part of the profession but doesn't know how to make it in the field of PR.

While working on this book, we realised that there are countless men and women who have tirelessly shaped and elevated the PR profession, both in India and globally. Their stories, too, deserve to be captured. These individuals have inspired generations of professionals, created immense value for clients and provided employment opportunities for many. While it wasn't possible to include all these stories in this book, we have launched a platform called 'Light a Spark' to ensure that these stories of inspiration continue to spread far and wide.

This book is the first phase of the Light a Spark project. We have called it *Spark* because in each of them there was a spark that created light, leading to the many success stories.

The additional stories of new-age founders and professional CEOs running PR firms will be captured in an e-book called *Shine*. This will be followed by insights from in-house communication leaders as well. We have categorised these four sets of people as 'Pioneers', 'Captains', 'Frontrunners' and 'Guardians'.

Over time, we hope this initiative will grow across multiple facets, including a conclave that will inspire the next generation of PR professionals. Visit www.lightaspark.online to read more.

It is our hope that this book will inspire, shape and empower you in some way, perhaps even making you a better person or professional. This is a passion project. It is a gift from us to the PR community and to anyone who wishes to learn from the journeys of those who came before them.

We want to go back a few years to share some more perspective. The thought first occurred to Sarika in 2019, when she wanted to get twenty leaders to pen a case study each, from which others would learn. That idea was a work in progress when things went haywire across the world because of the COVID-19 pandemic. In the last couple of years, Sarika has been reading one book every month and reviewing it to help PR professionals to benefit from the same. She has done forty-two reviews and counting as of September 2024. Last year, Amith co-authored a book with Sujit Patil, which had over seventy-five leaders also sharing short essays across chapters, much like this one. This was considered useful literature by many in the profession. *The Pursuit of Reputation*, also published by Westland, showed that there was a need for more such books.

We also realised that we were on a 'giving back' spree. We had created Sparkle Gift Cards in 2023, and it was time to create something unique in 2024. Thus, the project Light a Spark was born. While there could be grammatical doubts about the name—how do you Light a Spark? You ignite a spark and light a fire—we took the liberty of calling it this way.

Some founders we reached out to refused to take part in this project as they prefer to keep their life private, and we respect their decision. Some others only wanted to share one or perhaps two of the three proposed sections in each chapter, and we were fine with that.

We decided to feature twenty-four of the 100+ professionals we spoke to in a printed book, and that is what you are holding in your hands. This will serve as a textbook for students, as a book of inspiration for professionals and a testimony of the great achievements of these men and women. This will be a continuous project, with at least eight individuals profiled online every month over a period of time.

There could be some individuals that you feel should be featured here but are not. Sorry to disappoint you. Share these names with us on email at manager@promisefoundation.com with the subject line #LAS, and we will try and connect with them for a future online or print edition. Your feedback is always welcome.

Lastly, we have decided that proceeds from this book will go to the Section 8 company that we co-created with Roshan Alexander to fund its administrative expenses. We hope you make sparklegiftcards.com a way of life, because the name 'Spark' is inspired from this social impact venture.

With all our heart, we thank you for reading.

1

Sunil Agarwal

Founder of 20:20 Media, currently a contributing cartoonist with *The Times of India*

'In my professional life, the biggest advantage has been my deep understanding of media and technology.'

Getting into Public Relations by Accident

I was born in Allahabad and completed my schooling there. Later, I attended IIT Delhi (1979) for the undergraduate programme and then IIM Ahmedabad (1981) for my post-graduation. My first job was at the advertising agency Rediffusion, where I worked for a year. After that, I had the opportunity to join the magazine *Dataquest* as its first editor. This was a significant milestone in my career, because *Dataquest* was the first magazine in India to write about computers and tech. In this role, I networked with the entire computer industry, which was just beginning to take shape in 1982. Everyone who was notable in the IT industry during the early 1980s had some interaction with *Dataquest*. At that time, there were only about ten companies in the industry, most of which no longer exist today.

Later, I joined Wipro to be part of their software product organisation, marketing software in the US. I spent a year in 1988 as the marketing director for Apple's distributor in India. It was around this time that I began writing and publishing a series of books under the brand 20:20 Publishing. These books focused on offbeat careers for school and college graduates, such as fashion design and architecture, which were not as mainstream as engineering or medicine at the time. A company called 20:20 Media was incorporated for this purpose on 21 February 1989.

I persuaded a bright young Dinesh Bahal to join me in this venture. Dinesh was previously the editor of another computer magazine, *C&C*, so he too had a background in technology and media. This experience led to opportunities in consulting for technology companies. Around that time, we secured our first client, Lotus Development Corporation, which was a competitor to Microsoft Excel. We handled their marketing and corporate communications. Our consulting work primarily involved creating content for our clients. For instance, we developed franchisee manuals for Aptech. This was our focus in 1990—creating content for technology firms.

Another early client was Digital Equipment Corporation, for whom we managed media relations. We also handled some projects for AT&T and IBM. We scraped the barrel for small jobs that sometimes involved a huge amount of work—for peanuts.

While we initially focused on creating marketing communication materials, we soon began crafting press releases and organising press interviews, mainly targeting the trade press. It was only later that we realised this was all part of the larger umbrella of 'Public Relations', or PR. In fact, we didn't even refer to it as 'PR' at the time. We came to understand this field when we saw companies like Good Relations and IPAN doing similar work in India and being labelled as PR firms. This realisation led us to hire talent from these companies, which helped us acquire more clients. For about ten years, we remained focused solely on technology clients. When the dot-com boom happened, our business really took off.

In my professional life, the biggest advantage has been my understanding of media and technology. As the editor of a technology magazine, I further honed my understanding of technology and my network within the industry. My engineering background also gave me the confidence to navigate the tech world effectively. These two skills—media and technology—were pivotal in our becoming a technology PR firm.

My niche expertise, combined with the skills of those who worked with me, initially in book publishing and then in consulting, played a significant role in our success. My partner left in 1991, which was around the time we realised we were a PR firm. After he left, I continued to run the company on my own.

Eventually, MSL acquired a majority stake in 20:20 in 2010. Following that, 20:20 MSL was handled by a team far better at PR than I was. I attribute the success of 20:20 to talented individuals like Amrit Ahuja, Chetan Mahajan, Kiran Ray Chowdhury, Himani Semwal and Sharad Gupta. I may have been instrumental in hiring them and my name might be associated with the company, but they were the ones who truly built it. Full credit goes to them; and perhaps some to me for recognising their potential and bringing them on board.

My greatest impact on the PR profession came from having no prior knowledge about PR. My focus was on marketing technology by persuading people with the right content. It was my team of PR experts who transformed this into a successful PR business. Many of them now run their own successful PR firms (such as Maverick and 80-db), applying the principles we developed back then.

My main contribution was understanding that technology and media needed to be integrated and recognising that companies needed this integration. A pivotal moment for us was in 1992, when the then finance minister Manmohan Singh opened India to foreign companies. This influx of technology companies, all with their own PR departments, needed local PR partners. Many of these companies hired us.

If you ask me, I was simply in the right place at the right time, and I brought along a talented team who then worked their magic.

2

Atul Ahluwalia

Former Vice Chairman of Weber Shandwick India, currently Founding Partner, First Partners

'What sets us apart is our bifocal approach: balancing long-term brand reputation and immediate business outcomes.'

The Class Topper Who Made it in Public Relations

I was born and raised in New Delhi, completing my schooling at St. Columba's, where I consistently scored top marks. I then enrolled at Sri Ram College of Commerce. Instead of pursuing an MBA, I decided to become a chartered accountant (CA). However, I soon realised my heart was not in finance and considered career options in hotel management, advertising and the airline industry. Ultimately, I chose advertising and started working at a small design firm run by an expat called John Collington, whose clients included several PR firms such as IPAN and Mudra PR.

I started to gain insights into the world of PR while servicing IPAN and Mudra PR as clients. We created corporate identity manuals and brochures, alongside supporting these consultancies with various creative communication materials. This involvement gradually drew me to the PR profession. Venu Menon, head of client servicing at IPAN, took a liking to me. He was tasked with setting up the Delhi office of a new PR firm called Corporate Voice and discussed the possibility of me working for him.

I had an interview scheduled with JWT, the top advertising agency at the time, for an account executive position. Meanwhile, Venu was offering me the role of an account manager. For a week, I was unsure about which offer to take. Advertising was well-established, but at JWT, I would have to compete with many others to stand out. PR, on the other hand, was a nascent profession. How far it would grow was uncertain at the time, but I believed that with hard work, I could make a significant impact.

Despite a lower salary offer, I chose PR because it was a new profession, and I was comfortable joining a smaller team. In retrospect, I am happy with my decision, as it has paid off very well. I never looked back, and perhaps because I had lost some time earlier, I was even more determined to prove myself. Within four years, I was made the head of the Delhi office and eventually became the national head of the firm. I worked at Corporate Voice for about twenty-one years. During this period, the firm became Corporate Voice Weber Shandwick and was subsequently rechristened Weber Shandwick. I am proud that my business partner Dilip Yadav and I made Weber Shandwick the most awarded PR firm in India.

The reasons we wanted to start our own firm were several. Firstly, while everyone talks about reputation management, we felt it was essential to work another track as well: business outcomes. Building a strong reputation takes years and requires effort and attention. However, clients are also under pressure to perform on their business goals and drive business outcomes. It was the business outcome focus that uniquely interested us. The tools for reputation building are different from those needed for driving business outcomes.

I believe PR will be taken seriously in boardrooms only if company leaders see a direct impact on their business. One way to achieve this is by making PR professionals excel at public policy communication, as many high-stake business outcomes lie at the intersection of public policy and PR. I felt the time was ripe for elevating PR beyond media relations.

At our firm, we blend public policy communication strategies with core PR services, making our proposition more material. We also excel at supporting marketing strategies and customer engagement. PR firms often fail to tailor tactics and messaging for specific audience groups. At our firm, we create bespoke tactics for each target audience segment to drive business outcomes more effectively.

Our approach combines creativity and analytics, a mix that has helped us consistently clinch awards and recognition. My personal strength in creativity and my co-founder Dilip Yadav's brilliance with analytics, along with the media prowess of my other co-founder, Santanu Gogoi, create a powerful combination that drives our success.

We prefer to work on holistic campaigns rather than piecemeal projects. It's crucial to bring everything together under one cohesive strategy. This ensures that all activities are aligned and contribute to the end goals. We put in a lot of effort to build a solid blueprint for our campaigns, which is more than just a standard communication plan—it's a fully integrated effort. This approach excites us, though it can be quite exhausting.

When we started, we had immediate support from leading brands like ITC and Rolls-Royce, as we had worked with the communication leaders of these companies before. All our other clients were new acquisitions. Our strong market reputation and being the most awarded team at that time certainly helped us build equity in the market and attract these clients.

Dilip, Santanu and I founded the firm together, and many former colleagues who were senior leaders at Weber Shandwick India soon joined us. Bringing our team together was effortless, as we had all worked closely for over a decade and shared a strong camaraderie—a spirit we continue to cherish to this day.

One campaign I would like to highlight is the one we worked on for Mangaldeep, a leading incense stick brand from ITC Limited, which is known for its leadership in sectors such as hotels, foods and personal care products. This campaign aimed to drive behaviour change among Indians towards waste segregation by using temples as the focal point. This was based on the insight that temples are the most frequented places in India with high-density crowds, and people are at their most pious in temples, making them more open to behaviour change. Changing citizens' attitude and behaviour towards waste segregation is one of the key goals of the Swachh Bharat Mission.

Direct communication and innovation around making manure as prasadam and cleaning as seva helped drive strong results and received overwhelming support from temple authorities. This led to high demand for the programme and a spike in sales for Mangaldeep. The campaign was so successful that it expanded from three temples to sixty-three major temples across India, who joined the programme to help manage waste and maintain cleanliness. 'Temple Run' became a highly awarded campaign, and an excellent example of the power of combining social initiatives with brand promotion.

Another notable campaign was for Hyundai, celebrating its twenty-fifth anniversary, coinciding with India's remarkable progress over the past twenty-five years. India is now on the verge of becoming, if not already, a superpower. Hyundai decided to mark this milestone with a dual celebration: twenty-five years of their successful presence in India and twenty-five years of India's remarkable socio-economic transformation.

To highlight this, Hyundai's annual property in India, called the 'Hyundai Great India Drive', became the perfect vehicle to take twenty-five leading journalists to twenty-five different locations in India to capture twenty-five stories of growth that encapsulated the company's vision of 'Progress for Humanity'.

For example, touching stories included a naturalist and conservationist making Jim Corbett National Park more sustainable, efforts to transform Dehradun into a smart city, and women entrepreneurs who moved from the US to Rajasthan to start social enterprises. This campaign, with its compelling stories and travelogues featuring Hyundai cars, resonated deeply with the audience and won several awards.

From Print to Pixels: PR Over the Last Two Decades

PR in India has undergone a significant transformation over the past two decades, reflecting broader socio-economic changes, technological advancements and evolving media landscapes. The evolution of PR in India is marked by a shift from traditional practices to a more dynamic, integrated and strategic approach.

At the turn of the millennium, PR in India was focused on media relations. The primary goal was to secure media coverage through press releases, press conferences and media events. Print media and television were the main channels for disseminating information. PR professionals maintained close relationships with journalists and editors, leveraging connections to gain favourable coverage for their clients. The approach was largely reactive and event-driven, with an emphasis on creating awareness rather than strategic communication.

By the mid-2010s, the profession had evolved into a more integrated and strategic function. Organisations recognised the need for a cohesive communication strategy that aligned PR with marketing, advertising and corporate communications. Integrated communication campaigns became the norm, leveraging multiple channels to convey a consistent message.

The role of PR professionals expanded beyond media relations to include strategic planning, stakeholder management and corporate social responsibility (CSR) initiatives. The rise of analytics and data-driven decision-making also transformed PR practices, enabling professionals to measure the impact of their campaigns and refine their strategies based on insights and metrics.

From the late 2010s, the digital landscape has matured, and PR practices in India have become more sophisticated. Digital news platforms, blogs and podcasts have diversified the media ecosystem, providing PR professionals with more avenues to reach their audiences. The focus has shifted to strategic storytelling, where compelling narratives are crafted to engage and resonate with target audiences.

Content creation has become central to PR strategies, with an emphasis on quality and authenticity. Video content, podcasts and interactive media have gained prominence, catering to the preferences of digital-savvy audiences. Social media platforms continue to play a crucial role, but with a more nuanced approach to community building and engagement.

Despite significant advancements, PR in India faces challenges such as media fragmentation, fake news and evolving audience expectations. The need for transparency and ethical communication has never been greater, with stakeholders demanding authenticity and accountability from organisations.

Looking ahead, the future of PR in India will likely be shaped by technological innovations such as artificial intelligence, augmented reality and big data analytics. These technologies have the potential to further enhance PR practices, enabling more personalised and impactful communication.

The Future of Influence: Navigating PR in a Machine-centric World

As India progresses towards becoming the world's third largest economy, the Indian PR landscape is poised for significant transformation. This economic surge, coupled with technological advancements and evolving consumer behaviours, presents both opportunities and challenges that necessitate a forward-thinking approach to communication, stakeholder engagement and reputation management. In this context, PR professionals must adapt and be able to craft narratives that resonate locally while also appealing to international audiences.

PR-tech will become mainstream—artificial intelligence (AI) will go beyond content.

AI, machine learning and augmented reality (AR) are going to revolutionise PR practices. AI will help precision in data analysis, automate routine tasks and help personalise content at scale. These advances will ultimately help PR professionals to focus on strategy and creative execution rather than on energy-sapping mundane tasks. At the other end of the same tech plane, AR, alongside virtual reality (VR) headsets, has the potential to completely change the way audiences 'experience' a brand through seamless immersive experiences. This can revolutionise event management and product launches.

Another notable shift in the PR landscape will be the adoption of data-driven strategies. Leveraging data to customise messages and distribution strategies will become essential. This approach will enable PR professionals to deliver more personalised and impactful content, enhancing engagement with diverse audiences.

Landscape of fragmented media—influencers take centre stage.

As the evolution of citizens into both consumers and creators of content intensifies, the media environment will become increasingly complex. This will lead to a shift in the balance of power, where large media platforms and niche communities co-exist. Influencers will gain greater prominence, playing an important role in shaping public opinion and brand narratives. As a result, PR strategies will need to encompass both platforms with wide reach and highly targeted community engagement.

Regional language content will build authentic connections.

In a multilingual country like India, the role of regional language communication cannot be underestimated. Brands will need to think from the ground up, embracing regional language content to ensure their messages resonate across various linguistic landscapes. This localised approach will be crucial in building authentic connections with diverse demographic segments.

Brands as publishers—companies will create more sophisticated newsrooms.

As the battle for control of communication intensifies, brands will more readily don the role of publishers. This phenomenon, already visible, will grow exponentially, and PR professionals will need to take greater responsibility for their content, redefining the traditional PR model and blurring the lines between media and brands.

CEO communicators—these leaders will provide more personalised brand communication.

The role of CEOs will also undergo a dramatic transformation. In an era of increased transparency, the distinction between private life and boardroom boundaries will blur. CEO social media handles will replace traditional company websites as primary sources for strategic insights. This change will necessitate a more authentic and personalised communication style from corporate leaders.

Purpose and trust will gain more currency.

As global challenges grow, such as environmental sustainability and social inclusion, the focus of communication will shift from merely telling the brand story to addressing the brand's response to these challenges. Corporate social responsibility (CSR) and purpose-driven narratives will take centre stage, reflecting the growing consumer demand for brands to contribute positively to society.

PR will help adapt public policy to new changes.

As technology and societal dynamics evolve rapidly, public policy must adapt to stay effective and relevant. PR professionals are expected to play an increasing role in this integration, leveraging their expertise in crafting compelling narratives and engaging diverse audiences to support and promote policy initiatives. Effective communication will be crucial in bridging the gap between policymakers and citizens, ensuring that policy changes are understood, accepted and effectively implemented at all levels of society.

3

Madan Bahal

Co-founder and Managing Director of Adfactors PR

'Learning from life, for life!'

From the Family Grocery Shop to Building India's Largest PR firm

I was born in 1956 in a fishing village called Govandi on the outskirts of Mumbai. This is where my childhood was spent. The simplicity, integrity and generosity of the villagers had a lasting impact on me. Without my knowing, they seeped into my consciousness. My childhood was spent playing in vast open areas with mango, tamarind and jamun trees besides running on dry paddy fields. We also had ambe wadis and chikoo wadis (fruit orchards) to learn climbing in. The village wells and ponds were where we learnt swimming.

The family grocery shop taught me early lessons in business. Very hardworking, honest and generous parents shaped my personality. For most of his life, my father worked two shifts in the docks, where he was a crane operator and later a foreman. On the weekends and whenever else he had time off, he attended to the grocery shop. I don't remember him *ever* taking leave until he retired due to health reasons. My mother managed the home with five kids and managed the grocery shop. My second lesson of a 'never, ever give up' attitude came from them.

I was an average student but very curious about everything. After school, I studied chemistry and physics at the undergraduate level.

Confession—in my university days, I was active in student politics!

After graduating in chemistry, the jobs available were that of a chemist, plant operator or medical representative. I preferred the latter, so I applied to multiple pharma companies, including Lupin and Wockhardt. While I cleared all the tests and interviews, the stumbling block was my refusal to wear a tie, which was mandatory for a medical representative. I refused three job offers, one after the other.

Pig-headedness or fierce independence? You decide!

This was followed by three brief stints between 1979 and 1981, about a year each, in market research (field work), advertising and media space selling. Each experience contributed to what followed. I must admit I was a quick learner. While working as a freelance investigator with a couple of leading research firms, I read available literature on research techniques. But I also took permission from the firm to read the 600-odd reports of the research projects the firm had conducted since it started!

In the ad agency, as a trainee account executive, I read every single physical file *across* departments, not just my own! Be it client servicing, media, creative, studio or production. This included all the presentations made and proposals submitted over many years.

The last stints, with the publications *Blitz* and *The Daily*, provided valuable lessons in the workings of the media. In each of these jobs, I realised I ended up challenging established notions and pushed myself and everyone around me to think differently.

The Launch of Adfactors Advertising: Putting the values to test

I launched Adfactors Advertising on 5 September 1981 with a capital of ₹450 in a village called Kapurbawdi outside the municipal limits of Thane city. A friend who owned a security services company generously granted me a small eighty-square-foot office. Our physical assets were two rented tables and four chairs. For external communications, we had a public telephone booth located sixty metres away. (Mobile phones came to India in 1995!)

Day 1 at Adfactors Advertising was very busy and very productive. With a writing pad and a pen, I started on my business development journey. Thane was an industrial area, and Wagle Industrial Estate was a huge complex of small and mid-sized factories. I chose one lane and entered the first office of a very small unit called Gala Springs. I was given the task of releasing a classified ad in *The Times of India* for 'turners and fitters'.

The second visit to a unit called Plastiblends resulted in a job for a product brochure. On that very morning, a visit to a third company called Micro Steel Treatments resulted in an advertisement for the industrial ads page of *The Times of India*. The most important omen that evening ... Adfactors signed up Monis, the first Grade One restaurant in Thane. They stayed with Adfactors for decades!

Day 1 set the confidence for the times to come

Two years later, after the early success, we moved to a small office in Fort, Mumbai, to be in the thick of the action. Our client portfolio expanded to retail and even some small consumer durable products.

In 1986, we managed our first IPO by chance. It received a sub-optimal response from the market, but the lessons were invaluable—both in terms of capital market communications and dealing with the trauma of a sub-optimal outcome for the client.

Let me take one step backwards.

Adfactors Advertising: The better half joins

In November 1984, Rajesh Chaturvedi (whom I had known since 1978) left his job as the head of advertising sales at *Blitz* and joined as my partner. Rajesh, who hails from Agra and has a distinct Lucknowi andaaz, had previously worked at *The Indian Express*. He became a deep influence on my life: he taught me to be tolerant, generous and gentle.

The two of us were, and continue to be, dramatically different personalities ... but bound by mutual love, respect, blind trust and a commitment to work together until we can work no more.

I am a dehaati; he is a style icon. I grew up playing village level lezhim and kho-kho, while Rajesh played hockey at the university and national level until a knee injury stopped his sports journey. I was cut and dry in my relationships, while Rajesh establishes relations effortlessly and holds them for life.

The trust and relationship capital Rajesh enjoys with the media and large family-owned clients of Adfactors is unparalleled. I believe I may have done some great karma in my past life to be blessed with a partner like Rajesh Chaturvedi.

Adfactors: The IPO journey kicks off

In 1988, a very happy client, SM Dyechem Limited, insisted that we manage their large ₹300 crore IPO to fund an ethanol plant. Mr S.M. Shetty, the chairman of SM Dyechem, and Mr O.P. Chaturvedi, the finance director, actively championed our cause with the investment bankers who were insisting on an experienced IPO advertising agency.

Their trust in us opened a path of lifelong opportunities for us—we are eternally grateful to them. The SM Dyechem IPO was a huge success, which also stirred the market for our sheer creative brilliance in IPO communications. Two more IPOs followed from the SM Group, giving us the credentials for bigger and more strategic projects.

The inflection point

In 1993, we worked on the tax-free bonds offer of Konkan Railway. In my opinion, it is probably *the* case study in managing complex communication goals through an integrated communications and stakeholder engagement programme in India!

Allow me to explain.

A quick summary of objectives: Quickly changing adverse perceptions, overcoming 'inspired' activism and marketing an unfamiliar product ('bond') to the investing public.

The campaign elements: Six different advertising campaigns running concurrently, mobilising the open and public support of India's most trusted influencers across all walks of life, personally engaging CFOs of 400 cash-rich corporations, 350 co-operative bank chairpersons in Maharashtra, Goa and Karnataka, and finally a door-to-door advocacy campaign that engaged 16,500 chartered accountants with a personal flipchart presentation across sixty-two towns in eleven states of India.

There is more unheard of, out-of-the-box stuff!

We mobilised the support of nearly 2,000 'Shetty-owned' restaurants to display the bond issue collateral. We identified an opportunity to leverage the railway network to amplify the campaign. We created jingles and provided them to the Indian Railways, who played them through their public announcement systems across the network.

Last but not the least, we made personal landline telephone calls to 65,000 households with 350 chosen surnames from coastal Maharashtra, Goa, Karnataka and Kerala!

At the cost of sounding self-congratulatory, this is a simple explanation of what makes Adfactors tick: commitment to resolute, purposeful, dogged, single-minded *execution*.

The success of the Konkan Railway bond issue didn't go unnoticed. The campaign was widely praised, and *The Economic Times* carried a six-column article on the front page describing the campaign and its success.

By 1995, Adfactors Advertising had found a leadership position in Prime Rankings, a highly credible data service that publishes league tables for capital market intermediaries. Twenty-nine years later, we have held the pole position, year after year, for volume of capital raised and/or the number of IPOs.

As the financial communications journey was gathering steam, massive changes were impacting the Indian business ecosystem. The reforms process initiated by the then Prime Minister P.V. Narasimha Rao's government unleashed structural changes in the Indian economy. These had a profound effect on the capital markets as well. The capital market regulator (the Securities and Exchange Board of India, or SEBI, founded in April 1988) was driving significant changes for an orderly market. The National Stock Exchange (NSE) began operations in 1993, followed by the foundation of National Securities Depository Limited (NSDL) in 1996.

These changes had an impact on our work as well. PR was becoming a critical tool for financial communications.

Several pioneering founders had already set up successful PR firms: Roger Pereira Communications in 1986; Genesis (Prema Sagar) in 1992; Perfect Relations (Dilip Cherian and Bobby Kewalramani) and Sampark (N.S. Rajan) in 1994; Clea (Sunil Gautam and P. Venugopal) in 1995.

Adfactors PR: The inception

Their early successes inspired us to launch Adfactors PR on Friday, 5 September 1997.

Exactly like in my advertising days, I spent the nine days before the launch reading and glancing through *all* the PR books in the library of KC College of Management Studies. A sort of a professional Navratri!

On day one, Rajesh and I approached Mr Ramesh Pilani, the founder of Ganesh Benzoplast, who had been an IPO client. We asked him for his PR business and he instantly signed us on a retainer of ₹50,000 per month.

In the following months, many large clients like Enron and ABN Amro Bank were signed up on retainers. In 1999, we expanded our group laterally: by launching India's first pure-play brand consultancy (as opposed to a design consultancy). That was how chlorophyll was born.

chlorophyll celebrated its twenty-fifth anniversary in 2024 by launching two seminal books on branding, based on the 400 brands it has been involved in!

Adfactors PR: Trial by fire

What started largely as a media relations and financial PR firm received its first major jolt in 2008 with the Lehman Brothers collapse, which snowballed into a global economic crisis.

Within the first three months, nearly 45 per cent of our clients suspended work or significantly reduced our fees, completely shaking up our business model, which was then dependent on a single vertical.

In the early days of the crisis, we called an open house, promising full job security through the crisis, mobilising all hands on the deck to deal with the storm and announcing our decision to diversify into other practices and verticals.

The collective hard work of the team helped us close FY2009 with a revenue growth of 5 per cent. We had kept our offices open day and night to cater to our domestic and international clients in the extreme environment of uncertainty.

Once the crisis was over, the experience inspired us to launch a new practice called Crisis 24x7, which was quickly followed by IPO Nurture, a specialist offering to build brand capital long before a company hit the capital markets.

By 2011–12, we had emerged as a front runner in the Indian PR business. Over time, we expanded our portfolio to include other practices and services to become a multi-specialist firm. The recent service offerings like Frontier Technologies, Mobility, New Energy, ESG and Social Impact caught the market imagination and have grown to become viable businesses.

Growth by design

We have been blessed by India Inc. Over the last fifteen years, we have had the privilege of serving the largest and most respected conglomerates in the corporate world, including Mahindra, L&T, Hinduja, Godrej, Tata, Aditya Birla, Piramal, Adani, Vedanta, TVS and parts of Murugappa Group.

It's a privilege and a challenge to be alive at a time like this!

Our clients and we have witnessed the digital explosion that allows every stakeholder of every corporate to voice their demands, every minute, every hour, every day.

We are at a technological inflection point with AI; economic volatility because of the COVID-19 disruption; geopolitical complexity because of multiple flashpoints; social divisions because of misinformation on social media.

So we have invented the concept of Complexity Counsel that factors in the scale, complexity and speed of change.

Corporate spirituality as the way ahead

We adopted and practised a value system early on in our lifecycle. A value system not just for our employees or clients, but for society, for the nation, for the earth.

Freedom, transparency, integrity, hard work, simplicity, client-centricity and continuous learning define our culture, internally and externally.

But knowing what not to do is as important as knowing what to do—don't lie, don't hurt, don't work for businesses engaged in tobacco, alcohol, gambling and meat processing, which doesn't align with my personal beliefs, or product categories like colas, which we consider harmful to society and the earth.

The future is both daunting and exciting … for every single stakeholder, internal and external. There is looming existential threat or exponential opportunity, depending on how we respond as a firm.

Both as an individual and as a firm, my belief is this challenge can only be answered by the concept of corporate spirituality: where each one of us arrives to work 'undivided', committed to doing good, both in business and in life.

Changing at the Speed of Light

'The price of doing the same old thing is far higher than the price of change.'—Bill Clinton

The world has changed more in the past five years than in the past five hundred. The same goes with India.

India's market capitalisation has grown exponentially, from $115 billion in April 1999 to $5 trillion in April 2024. Indian businesses have risen into powerhouses: growing close to a hundred times in twenty-five years.

The PR profession sits at the intersection of everything significant happening in the world, the nation and its businesses. Has it changed?

The pace of change impacting our work as PR consultants is an ever-accelerating bullet train. The PR profession is trying to catch up by *running* after the train, huffing and puffing along the tracks. The impact of this differential is evident all over. In 2023, the PRovoke Media annual consultancy ranking reported a mere 0.5 per cent growth of the global consultancy business. A large number of firms had negative growth with squeezed margins. Closer home, many top firms in the Indian PR ecosystem have experienced flat revenues and declining margins in the last five years.

How is this possible in a country like India which has high GDP growth and capital markets rising to new heights every month?

Hypothesis: PR professionals can't cope with the cataclysmic changes in the mediascape. Let me present a few proof points.

Earned influence—the raison d'être of PR has evolved from traditional media relations to a world of a million influencers and micro-influencers in our own country.

Consider just one dimension of the digital influence explosion in India: YouTube alone has over 75,000 channels with a subscriber base of over 1,00,000 each. A single YouTuber talking on issues like business or capital markets has a subscriber base many times higher than the combined circulation of all the business newspapers and magazines. Add to this AI and its applications like ChatGPT: '2029 is the consistent date I have predicted for when an AI will pass a valid Turing test and therefore achieve human levels of intelligence,' says Ray Kurzweil, the seer who has predicted most technology breakthroughs right for over two decades.*

Consider a totally unexpected dimension affecting our profession: global warming. The Southwest Monsoon, the lifeline of Indian agriculture and one of the most predictable weather systems in the world, is showing signs of disruption. The summer of 2024 recorded the highest ever temperatures in over a hundred Indian cities. Consider inequality: India's top 1 per cent income share is among the very highest in the world.

The PR consultancy and the PR practitioner, in India and in the world, has to find a new paradigm, a new algorithm, a

* Dom Galeon and Christianna Reedy, 'Robots will be smarter than us by 2029', *Sustensis*, 5 October 2017, https://sustensis.co.uk/robots-will-be-smarter-than-us-all-by-2029/.

new multivariate analysis that empowers them to factor in all the changes at all velocities.

As mentioned earlier, I have invented a concept for that paradigm: Complexity Counsel.

Existential Threats versus Exponential Opportunity

Crystallum aspicientes. That's Latin for crystal gazing. Crystal gazing is a risky business. Only fools indulge in long-range forecasting, according to a very wise man. Navigating the future is like navigating a river. One can only see until the next bend ... and be prepared for surprises around the next bend.

What is visible now in the PR river? A range of factors that will have a bearing on our profession and the business.

Factor 1

Technology impact. The impact of technology, particularly AI tools: a no-brainer.

For all the narratives being floated about the benign nature of AI, we have to come to terms with the impact on most white-collar jobs, including professional services. From software services to healthcare, from law firms to consulting, from advertising to media to PR, a potential tsunami of redundancy is on its way. Fewer employees may be required, and there may be a deflation of wages in roles with repetitive tasks and content generation.

The (unprepared) PR practitioner, perpetually complaining about the lack of a seat at the decision-making table, may be further marginalised. There is only one new seat available for the PR professional. The seat that says, 'I can help your company navigate complexity of all types.'

That's why I mentioned Complexity Counsel: making sense of the situation; proactive intelligence; offering custom solutions beyond the standard toolkit; ability to deal with the new influence paradigms—that's the new survival kit for businesses.

The opportunity for consulting has finally been delivered by market forces.

Factor 2

Consolidation. While acquisition by networks cooled off in the last couple of years, new categories of players are driving consolidation. These are the private equity players aggregating PR firms to build scale or large law firms and consulting firms adding a PR / Investor Relations (IR) firm to their offering.

Recent high-profile examples include the investment in the Swiss PR firm, Framer, by Meritech Capital, to build a pan-European platform. Another is the acquisition of Europe's leading public affairs firm Interel by the law firm Dentons. The acquisition of WPP stake in FGS Consulting at a valuation of $1.7 billion by KKR is another example of this.

Over time, I expect PR firms will go for listings.

Factor 3

Investments. Client–consultancy relationships and the remuneration models are overdue for change in India (and around the world!). There are a number of new value-added services that will have to be outside the fixed retainer model. Myriad reputational challenges and critical issues will necessitate an increase in budget allocations, both in-house and for the consultancy.

In India, the average monthly retainer of $5,000 simply isn't enough to manage reputation risks in a digitally empowered country of 140 crore people, unmatched socio-cultural-political diversity, thousands of newspapers and television channels, low journalistic rigour and slow judicial redressal for reputational harm.

Existential threats? Or exponential opportunity? Indian PR consultancies stand on the razor's edge. Those who are quick to adapt and evolve may be around to witness the continuing drama.

There is a lot of misattribution in what Charles Darwin actually said, but let me end with what I think makes common sense: 'According to Darwin's *On the Origin of Species*, it is not the most intellectual of the species that survives; it is not the strongest that survives; but the species that survives is the one that is able best to adapt and adjust to the changing environment in which it finds itself.'

Rajesh Chaturvedi is a co-founder and chairperson of Adfactors PR. He prefers not to be profiled. We respect his request. Some of his career trajectory is covered in the chapter above.

4

Manisha Chaudhary

Joint Group COO and Co-Founder of V360 Group

'Every interesting story and idea converting into something tangible and yielding results gives me a real sense of satisfaction and excitement.'

The Seeds of Entrepreneurship Were Sown Early On

Reflecting on my life, I realise that everything seems to have happened serendipitously; nothing was meticulously planned.

I was born in Moradabad, Uttar Pradesh, into a close-knit family of five that included my father, mother, brother and sister. My family had a business background and was always very traditional. Growing up, I saw the women in my family take up responsibilities within the home, familial duties being their priority. I, on the other hand, aspired to test the waters in the outside world and build a career in an upcoming field.

My father had an established import–export business in Moradabad. Seeking better opportunities, he decided to move to Delhi, where the property market was evolving rapidly. So, in the late seventies, our family started afresh in a new city. I studied at Darbari Lal D.A.V Model School (DLDAV) in North Delhi. Throughout my schooling, I put in consistent effort and developed a wide range of interests, though I often found myself contemplating what the future would hold for me.

Looking back, I believe this was when the seeds of entrepreneurship were planted in me. I was deeply inspired by my father's resilience and determination to rebuild and grow his business in a new city. His entrepreneurial spirit and ability to navigate challenging circumstances left a lasting impression on me, instilling in me a drive to pursue my own business path, which I would later discover.

For a long time, my goal was simply to earn some money due to the financial struggles I had witnessed in my family from a young age. Watching my parents work tirelessly to ensure we had access to education and basic necessities instilled in me the importance of hard work and gratitude. I learnt that no matter the situation, you can't afford to become complacent. This understanding grew stronger as I reached eleventh and twelfth grade, knowing that our struggles were far from over and that I needed to figure out my career path.

After completing school, I unexpectedly ventured into mass communication. At the time, Indraprastha University was expanding rapidly, and several new colleges were emerging. I took an entrance exam for a bachelor's in business administration, unaware that it was combined with mass communication. During the course orientation, a professor introduced us to the innovative and dynamic field of mass communication. It sounded novel and exciting, so I decided to embrace this opportunity.

Coming from a business-oriented family, I had little awareness of the media field. Venturing into mass communication was a turning point for me. Moving from North Delhi to South Delhi exposed me to a diverse group of students and broadened my horizons. I learnt about cinema, TV reporting and PR, although PR was a minor part of the curriculum at the time. Most of my peers pursued careers in television or filmmaking, with some achieving significant success, like Guneet Monga, who went on to win an Oscar.

But, for me, it was always going to be PR. In hindsight, it is evident that every step I have taken has contributed to my journey in PR. During my graduation, I started tutoring students, which taught me the nuances of training. I later applied these at Value 360. In college, I also organised promotional events, gaining valuable experience in engaging with and pitching ideas to diverse individuals. It's interesting to see how various experiences in life can shape and prepare you for the future. It was like everything was leading me to this profession, this company and this life.

After my bachelor's degree, I landed a stint at Jain TV, where my role was to cover the latest news stories. However, I felt my academic journey was not yet complete. While I was still figuring out my next steps in terms of higher education, I came across a course in development communication at Jamia Millia Islamia's Mass Communication Research Centre (MCRC). This course focused on documentary filmmaking, video editing and sustainability. I was excited about the prospect of creating and editing videos and enrolled in the course.

Little did I know that here too I was learning key skills that would eventually help me in my PR journey. For instance, new concepts like corporate social responsibility (CSR) strategies and sustainability were first introduced to me during this course. Undoubtedly, these are key focus areas for brand building and reputation management today. The knowledge I gained then helps me create more comprehensive strategies that are impactful now.

While I was still completing the course, Kunal and his partners (two of our juniors in college), approached me to join their newly established firm. This promising new company was named Precision PR, and it marked the beginning of my journey in PR.

I initially thought of saying yes just to earn some pocket money and then move to Mumbai to try my hand at film-making or editing. However, I found myself enjoying the world of PR. Every interesting story idea converting into something tangible and yielding results gave me a real sense of satisfaction and excitement.

In the beginning, we were a small team of just four people, and our humble office space was alive with enthusiasm. We were all very eager, and there was an air of healthy competition among us. We were all just starting out and had the drive to learn as much as we could. No one was working in a silo or on anything particular—we were all doing everything. This was especially true of me—I was keen on learning new things about every domain and every aspect of PR, from planning media strategies for clients to determining the best approach for their media engagements. That end-to-end learning journey helped me and still continues to help me plan the best media outreach for clients.

While I was deeply interested in my work at Precision PR, I still felt a sense of confusion. Was video editing—the degree I had pursued—my true calling? Or was PR a long-term career option for me? This is when I reached out to a trusted professor from my college, admitting that the practical applications of PR were far removed from what our post-graduation coursework had explored. His response was invaluable. He suggested that I leverage my foundational knowledge and seize the opportunity to create something of my own at such a young age. He suggested I give it a few more years because he could see that I was developing a genuine interest in PR, which could turn into something substantial.

That is exactly how it played out. I found myself developing a strong curiosity and desire to explore multiple domains within PR. I took on projects in tech, hospitality and various others, each introducing me to new challenges and concepts. Interacting with the media and devising innovative strategies for my clients quenched my thirst for knowledge and continuous learning. With renewed motivation and satisfaction, I decided to stay in PR.

With my heart completely in it, I started experimenting with specific segments. The corporate and technology segments caught my interest, much more than the lifestyle sector. Precision PR, however, was being built as more of a lifestyle PR firm. As it happened, Kunal was approached by an old journalist friend who was looking to build a PR company that would cater more to corporates. We decided to switch lanes, step away from Precision PR and go into business with him. That friend was Gaurav Patra, and together the three of us laid the foundation for Value 360 Communications. When Gaurav joined us, he brought in a rich IT background, which further steered my focus towards corporate and technology PR. The rest, as they say, is history.

Since the beginning, Value 360 Communications went all out. We had the zeal and enthusiasm to prove ourselves in a market with a few huge players. We worked towards continuous growth and recognition through shared ideals and the will to succeed. We were a young, agile team with fresh ideas, and the start-ups we worked with were also young and eager to experiment with innovative ideas. Our lean team was able to execute these ideas quickly, which worked to our advantage. We understood the immediate needs of start-ups, especially during their initial phases, when gaining a lot of attention was crucial. We tailored our strategies to their growth stages, continuously innovating to meet their evolving requirements.

We weren't rigid about the scope of work. Instead, we were flexible and willing to go all out to give them the exposure they needed at different stages. I had a fantastic team back then, many of whom are still with us. We were quick with our ideas and execution, matching the agility that start-ups demanded.

We provided ideas that aligned with their growth. In the early days, when start-ups wanted to attract investor attention, we didn't just wait for them to give us something to execute. We dug deep, tried to thoroughly understand their business and created strategies that got them the right attention. It was a collaborative process. The start-ups were eager for our ideas and often helped refine them. This two-way interaction was crucial in driving our success with them.

I remember that the conversion rate for new business pitches was incredibly high back then. The start-ups we worked with saw excellent results from our efforts. We were converting nearly all the businesses our team pitched to, largely thanks to the strong word-of-mouth we had built through our exceptional work with companies such as Snapdeal. Another factor that helped us was that other, more established PR firms were not paying much attention to start-ups at the time, thinking that their hypergrowth was nothing more than a phase. We continued to evolve into a trusted communications partner for growing start-ups.

Today, my primary role is to maintain a healthy client retention ratio. Once a client comes on board, I step in to curate the right strategy for them, working closely with my team. I ensure all necessary hygiene checks are in place and handle escalations, if any.

Recently, we worked on a fascinating campaign for Bold Care, a company specialising in men's sexual wellness. This campaign was particularly interesting because we collaborated with various influencers and a scriptwriter, giving it a unique treatment to draw attention to men's sexual health, a topic that still faces a lot of stigma in society.

The campaign involved creating a dramatic and engaging narrative, essential to driving attention towards the product, given its distinct category. The founder, being young, understood that the traditional media approach wouldn't work. Simply asking the media to write about men's sexual wellness would be ineffective given the nature of the topic.

Instead, our strategy was to focus on the importance of the subject rather than directly selling the product. Men's sexual wellness is often kept under wraps because people are hesitant to discuss it openly. We aimed to change that by bringing it to the forefront in a way that would capture media interest and public attention.

The whole process, from planning to execution, was incredibly engaging. We scheduled one-on-one talks with a well-known personality famous for discussing sexual health topics. The innovative treatment of the campaign and its strategic planning made it a success.

What was particularly surprising was the campaign's reach. Even people in other countries watched the ad, showing the effectiveness and broad impact of our approach. Working on this campaign with my team was a rewarding experience.

Snapdeal was another notable client and was a veritable turning point in Value 360's journey. This was an initial feather in our cap—a start-up that practically built the online shopping category and grew into a unicorn, with us as their PR partner.

Building the entire category of online shopping involved driving a significant behavioural change. We were tasked with creating awareness of the concept from scratch, showing people that everything they needed was a click away. This transformation wasn't achieved in three months but was an ongoing process that unfolded over a longer period. Witnessing and contributing to this journey provided invaluable learning experiences for all of us. Our successful work with Snapdeal put us on the map with the investor community, and we saw an influx of start-ups seeking us out for long-term partnerships.

And then, there was the stark rise of PayTM during demonetisation. I believe everyone remembers this campaign like it was yesterday—'PayTM Karo' resonated with each and every consumer. For us, it was another pivotal case study that brought about monumental change, highlighting the power of strategic communication in times of major economic shifts.

From a One-Dimensional Field to an Unrecognisable Landscape

I have been a witness to the remarkable transformation of our profession over the past two decades, and I am in awe of how far we have come. PR has reshaped the way brands communicate and engage with their audiences. Twenty years ago, PR was largely a one-dimensional field, focused on media relations and press releases. With pure-play PR campaigns being the mainstay of the profession, securing coverage across traditional media outlets was our singular goal. Today, the landscape is veritably unrecognisable. We have evolved into a multifaceted discipline that integrates multiple communication channels into a cohesive strategy.

This change has primarily stemmed from the advent of digital technologies. From the era of online news portals to social media platforms, we have consistently democratised information distribution, moving beyond traditional routes. Today, there is a diverse array of platforms that we can utilise to reach our target audience. Social media platforms like X (formerly Twitter) and Instagram have transformed brand communication into a two-way dialogue and opened up avenues for interaction between stakeholders. This direct line between brands and stakeholders has increased the need for communication to be more authentic, transparent and meaningful. This has also challenged us to adapt our strategies time after time, allowing for innovation to continually drive us forward.

So, from pure-play PR, we have advanced to integrated campaigns that essentially blend PR with digital marketing, social media management and data analytics. The lines between these key marketing functions have blurred, leading to the need for PR professionals to develop a broader skillset and a more comprehensive understanding of the communications landscape.

The most significant change, perhaps, has been the rise of data-driven PR. With data analytics and AI tools, we now make more informed decisions and can measure impact with more accuracy than ever before. We also use analytic tools to gauge sentiment, track engagement and boost ROI in ways that were unimaginable twenty years ago. While AI has made routine tasks simpler and more efficient, it has also enhanced the need for a human touch in our campaigns and to build genuine relationships.

As we look to the future, it's clear that PR will continue to change at a rapid pace. Successful PR practitioners will thrive if they achieve and maintain a balance between technology and storytelling, incorporating innovation into their approach.

Yes, we have come a long way in twenty years, but I am more excited about the next twenty. There is a lot more to come.

An Era of Transformation

Over the years, the PR business has witnessed colossal transformation, and I believe that change is still underway. In the years to come, PR is poised to be more dynamic, comprehensive and, most importantly, indispensable. Driven by rapid technological advancements and fast-changing stakeholder expectations, the ecosystem is shifting towards its next phase of evolution.

The interconnected world is giving rise to a hyper-aware stakeholder base, with increased access to information from various channels. As brands and PR practitioners consider this factor, we will see the heightened importance of authenticity and transparency in the PR segment. Consumers will continue to demand honesty and clarity from the brands they engage with, and we will increase the focus on authentic, meaningful conversations to help brands build and maintain consumer trust.

Apart from authenticity, stakeholders and consumers are also increasingly concerned about the environmental and social impact of the brands they support. Integrating sustainability and CSR into communication plans will grow in importance. Clients will need to highlight their positive contributions to society and the environment, which will be crucial in enhancing their reputation and aligning with the values of modern consumers.

It is also exciting to predict how technology will tie into every facet of the PR landscape of tomorrow. The use of AI-powered tools, such as chatbots and predictive analysis, is revolutionising the way we formulate and conduct our campaigns. These technologies are already helping us analyse vast datasets both quickly and accurately, giving access to valuable insights into audience behaviour and preferences. We will see more PR teams using data and predictive analysis to anticipate trends and craft proactive strategies to create compelling campaigns that are precisely targeted and highly impactful.

The future of PR is both promising and complex. There are opportunities and challenges ahead of us, as the business evolves into a more tech-driven function that is strategically critical for businesses. As more businesses turn to PR to unlock sustainable success in a largely unpredictable business landscape, we will need to be adaptable and agile. Navigating ever-increasing communication channels with a tailored approach along with flexible strategies that can transcend platforms to connect with diverse stakeholders will ultimately drive PR forward in the years to come.

5

Kunal Kishore Sinha

Group CEO and Co-Founder of V360 Group

'My life in boarding school taught me resilience, independence and confidence, qualities essential for my future career.'

A Long Journey from Hazaribagh to New Delhi

I come from a business family. My father used to run a transport business in Jharkhand. I was born in and did my schooling up to the tenth grade from Hazaribagh, a small town in present-day Jharkhand. My childhood was a bit of a struggle, transitioning from a small town to a big city. I was one of the brightest in my extended family, excelling academically, especially in maths and science. My family hoped that I would be the first to crack the IIT entrance exam, since I consistently scored in the nineties.

In the eastern part of the country, most people are typically expected to pursue one of three career paths: IIT, that is engineering, medicine or an MBA, that is management. These were the options I was groomed to pursue. While I loved maths, I was also into performing arts, enjoying being on stage. This was a passion I wanted to pursue. I participated in plays, dances and debates, making a name for myself in my early school days in Hazaribagh. I attended St Xavier's School, which gave me a strong command over the English language, a significant advantage for a small-town boy.

After the tenth grade, I moved to Delhi to attend school at DPS Mathura Road. This shift happened because my father wanted me to have better opportunities to prepare for IIT JEE, the joint entrance exam to get into the prestigious institutes. In Delhi, I stayed in a boarding school, which was a significant change. The first two years in Delhi helped shape my personality and future career, though my academic performance declined—I scored only 67 in maths in the twelfth grade. Despite this, the life skills I gained in boarding school were invaluable. My life there taught me resilience, independence and confidence, qualities essential for my future career. It made me realise that everyone should experience boarding school, as it prepares you for life's ups and downs. My time there significantly influenced who I am today. With its peer learning and challenges, it shaped my ability to adapt and thrive in unfamiliar environments. While my academic performance suffered, the life skills I gained were crucial. My time in boarding school contributed significantly to making me the public person I am today.

These experiences prepared me for a career in PR, a field unknown to someone from Hazaribagh.

I have an extensive social network of friends, and I thrive on it. Each friend plays a different role in my life—some are sounding boards, some are cheerleaders and some keep me grounded no matter how successful I become. They help me stay balanced and support me in times of crisis.

As founders, we may often be lonely at the top, dealing with situations we can't discuss with our team or anyone else. That's where these friends come in; they become a sounding board, lending a ear and much-needed support. Sometimes, even family isn't the right audience for certain concerns, making these friendships even more valuable.

From boarding school to college and beyond, I have maintained this network. We lived in a boys' dorm after boarding school, further strengthening these bonds. This network extends into my professional connections as well.

I have friends from all walks of life—editors in the media sector, college mates who have won Oscars and Filmfare awards, a colonel in the army and even an agriculturist. This diversity is fascinating and essential because it provides a break from the monotony of work-related conversations. When you meet people from the same industry, discussions often revolve around work and the industry. But with friends from various fields, conversations are more personal, focusing on each other's lives rather than work.

Coming back to my academic years, my father believed that even if I had a year of distraction, my talent and intelligence couldn't be taken away. He encouraged me to keep trying, so I did. I would stay with friends, study for four hours, and then spend most of my time playing cards—not gambling, but playing a team game called 29—or watching TV. I ended up wasting two years. When everyone kept telling me that my intelligence would carry me through, I began to fool myself into thinking I didn't need to study as much as others.

Two years later, I met my cousin's friend Raj Kumar Gupta, who had been my local guardian when I was in Delhi. He had just returned from Bombay after completing a course at the Xavier Institute of Communication. He eventually became a film director, working on projects like *Mission Kashmir* and *Aamir*. He introduced me to the field of mass communication, which trains you for careers in entertainment and journalism. Intrigued, I discussed it with my father, who was always progressive and supportive.

I admitted to my father that I couldn't commit to intensive book study for twenty hours a day and preferred a more hands-on approach. After speaking with a few professionals, my father saw the potential in the emerging media and entertainment industry in India and encouraged me to pursue mass communication. I applied to IP University, which had just launched its first undergraduate course in mass communication. I was part of the inaugural batch at the Madhu Bala Institute of Communication and Electronic Media.

During those three years, I enjoyed the workshop-based activities like shooting documentaries, publishing newspapers and creating ad campaigns. I aspired to get into filmmaking. However, just before finishing college, my family faced a massive financial crisis. My father told me he couldn't sustain our expenses, including rent, mess fees and travel costs.

At that time, the BPO industry was booming, and companies in that sector were hiring every day. I decided to join a BPO to support myself and my sister. I started working at Daksh, handling inbound calls for a US telecom company's activation department. Their extensive training programmes helped me improve my language skills.

Around the same time, I started dating Manisha, who was pursuing her master's in video editing at Jamia Milia Islamia University. She suggested I consider a career switch. She felt that a long-term future in a call centre was unsustainable, especially with the night shifts. This prompted me to rethink my career path.

Manisha found an opportunity with a PR firm based in Bangalore that was opening a branch in Delhi. I had also been applying to other PR firms, trying to break into the profession. One of my friends, Piyush, who is now a client, was in the advertising world. I told him I wanted to get into advertising because I believed in my creative abilities. He suggested I meet his senior Arvind. We had a two-hour chat, during which Arvind asked if I had studied PR. I mentioned the three-month course I had taken. He encouraged me to explore the PR profession, noting its potential, even if it didn't have the glamour of advertising.

I interviewed at Perfect Relations, fresh out of college, with no real understanding of what PR entailed. They quizzed me on the national and city editors of *The Times of India*, which I didn't know. Although I didn't get through the interview, the Bangalore firm India Relations was desperate for someone because of the growing tech firms and trade media in Delhi. The founder saw potential in me due to my language skills and confidence and offered me the job.

At the time, I was earning ₹8,500 at the call centre and was worried about my expenses. I didn't leave my BPO job immediately. Instead, I juggled both jobs for three months, working at the PR firm from 10 a.m. to 6.30 p.m. and then heading to the BPO at night. The dual job routine took a toll on my health, and friends urged me to choose one of the two. Eventually, I left the BPO, relying on my savings to sustain me for a few months.

Unfortunately, shortly after I left the BPO, India Relations lost several clients and shut down their operations. Despite this setback, I learnt the basics of PR. Vidyaa, a promising manager, guided me on how to connect with journalists. I reached out to other consultancies—namely, Integral PR and Lexicon PR—and got offers from both. Lexicon offered a higher salary, but I was more interested in Integral because of their client roster. I requested Integral to match Lexicon's offer, but they couldn't, so I joined Lexicon.

At Lexicon, I was primarily a media executive but was eager to contribute to revenue generation. I started cold-calling companies that were hiring with ads in the job supplements of *The Times of India*. I identified these as potential clients. My first success was an air hostess academy, which led to more leads. However, my senior didn't acknowledge my contribution, which disappointed me. This motivated me to consider starting my own venture.

I started my first venture, Precision PR, with a friend who was a salsa dancer. He needed help building a brand profile for his salsa institute, and I offered my services. Manisha had completed her course by then, and some of my colleagues were interested in joining me. We pooled together our resources, including a laptop contributed by one partner's father, and rented a small space in Gulmohar Park, Delhi.

Our first big client was an after-school activity centre called Leap Year. To impress them, we quickly set up makeshift workstations and called friends to pose as staff. The client visited our office and was convinced by our setup. This client, with a monthly retainer of ₹50,000, marked the beginning of our journey.

This experience taught me the fundamentals of PR and demonstrated the importance of perseverance and creativity in building a successful business. Eventually, we parted ways, as I wanted to focus on corporate PR and my other partners wanted to continue with lifestyle PR.

Meanwhile, I met Gaurav Patra at *The Indian Express*, where he was the Delhi editor for *Express Computers*. He was very supportive and helped me connect with clients. Around the same time, he was planning to start his own PR firm. Interestingly, our paths crossed again when his partnership in another firm didn't work out. This led us to join forces and establish Value 360 Communications together. It felt like destiny that we were meant to start this venture, despite the initial challenges of understanding the importance of partnership and avoiding past mistakes.

Since then, we have been blessed with finding dedicated people who have become the pillars of our company. Having a good combination of founders is crucial, especially when two out of the three founders are also married to each other. Value 360 Communications was founded in February 2007, and Manisha and I got married in May 2007, marking the beginning of my entrepreneurial journey with Value 360.

Attracting big international brands or established family-owned businesses to work with us initially proved to be a challenge. Instead, we focused on new businesses entering the Indian market. In 2008, our trajectory changed dramatically when Snapdeal approached us. Initially, I had declined because they were in the business of offering a loyalty card with discounts at restaurants, which seemed outside our usual media landscape.

However, when we lost several retail clients after the fallout of the Lehman Brothers crisis, Kunal Bahl of Snapdeal came back with the same proposition, and we decided to take on the challenge. Within three months, Snapdeal transformed into an online marketplace and rebranded themselves. We played a pivotal role in shaping their public profile during this transformative period. Our success with Snapdeal led to recommendations from investors to other portfolio companies, and soon, start-ups like Urban Clap (now Urban Company), Practo, ShopClues and PayTM sought our services without us actively seeking them out.

This organic growth also opened doors with established businesses. For instance, BMW engaged us for regional PR projects, which expanded our expertise into the automotive sector. Today, our portfolio includes a diverse range of clients, from cars and two-wheelers to EV start-ups and auto tech labs. Each step along the way contributed to shaping who we are today, sequentially building our reputation and expertise in the business.

One defining campaign that everyone remembers is PayTM during the demonetisation period. At that time, PayTM wasn't the only wallet company; there were competitors like Mobikwik and FreeCharge. What set us apart was the ground-level work we did, which remains largely unknown.

We had a monitoring team not just tracking media coverage of PayTM, but also monitoring where cash shortages were most severe in different cities. For instance, if the Kolkata fish market closed due to lack of cash, our monitoring team would report this to the national merchant acquisition team. This information was then passed on to the regional teams, who onboarded merchants in those markets using QR codes. We then pitched these stories through our robust media relations network.

While competitors focused on engagement in major publications like *The Economic Times*, we went deeper, creating real user acquisition stories and positioning PayTM as an enabler rather than just a beneficiary. During demonetisation, with cash scarce and traditional payment methods limited, this strategy significantly helped PayTM.

In the two years following demonetisation, our efforts paid off. Vijay Shekhar Sharma, the founder of PayTM, celebrated the success of this initiative. During the annual day celebration, attended by 5,000 people, he recognised key contributors from both McCann and Value 360 for their crucial roles in this success. That holds a special place in our minds and hearts.

Decades of Shaping and Reshaping the Profession

I completed twenty years in the PR profession in March 2023, which gives me a unique vantage view of its evolution through the last two decades. I have spoken about this previously, and believe that the journey of PR can be divided into four distinct phases, where a massive change was seen every five years or so.

The first phase, 2003–08, was the era of media domination. A brand's perception was crafted by the media, and it was through this vehicle that brands connected with different stakeholders. At this juncture, brand communication was a monologue.

In the period 2008–13, we witnessed the second phase, driven by the emergence of social media. When Facebook was born in 2007, followed by the launch of Twitter and LinkedIn, there was a decided shift in PR dynamics. The monologue transformed into a multidimensional dialogue powered by social media. Now, brands had several outlets to directly connect with their audiences, and the consumers could actually respond. They could express their thoughts around the organisation or its products, giving brands specific feedback and direction. Brands were no longer just talking but also listening.

The years 2013–18 were fuelled by data. The PR landscape could now leverage the power of big data to gauge consumer sentiment, map campaign performance and alter their strategies accordingly. Data became the cornerstone of brand communications strategies across the globe, giving brands the power of informed, data-driven decision-making, which led to precision in all communication efforts.

The next phase of PR, 2019–23, will forever be etched in history as the time when the entire fraternity banded together against the impact of COVID-19. When the pandemic took the world by storm, we reoriented ourselves at lightning speed and catapulted tech adoption. Webinars, Clubhouse, Twitter Spaces, Instagram Lives and podcasts became the flavour of the day. There was a surge in digital platforms where brands could stay connected with their stakeholders even when the world had come to a grinding halt.

Which brings us to right now. I believe that the next phase of PR has begun. Today, we are living in the era of Artificial Intelligence (AI). The advancements in AI have allowed us to ramp up content creation, campaign optimisation and data-driven decision-making. We are able to offer more tailored experiences to our clients with the help of AI and deliver greater efficiency.

It is exciting to anticipate how this phase will unfold further, but one thing is for sure—AI will overturn the status quo and reshape the PR profession yet again.

An Indispensable Profession

In the near future, perhaps over the next five years, PR is set to become more indispensable and comprehensive than ever. The profession, as we know it, will transform far beyond the basics of AI technology and traditional tools, into a full-service stakeholder engagement function. The increasingly complex landscape of communication mediums and the expansive web of stakeholders that a business must engage with will make PR a critical function—even more critical than it is now. The transformation is already underway.

In the past, PR was primarily focused on amplifying business announcements and managing public perception in a linear manner. Today, the environment is far more complex—the consumers are fragmented. Their perceptions are influenced by several factors in the larger ecosystem and can change every minute. In such a scenario, mitigating reputational risk is no longer optional but essential. Crisis management, thus, will become a cornerstone of PR activities. PR teams will grow exponentially in importance to proactively safeguard brand reputation, anticipating and responding to crises in real time.

Looking ahead, PR will become as integral to businesses as accounting or legal services. It will take on a comprehensive consulting role, providing insights into diverse stakeholder management and best practices for engagement. This consulting role will also extend to advising brands about their CSR activities, sustainability efforts and similar initiatives, where stakeholder perception is vital. Here, advanced AI tools and data analytics will be essential to creating highly targeted and effective communication campaigns. These tools will also be required to keep continuous tabs on consumer sentiment, reach and engagement. Precision will be a mainstay of PR.

Moreover, PR is set to surpass traditional advertising in importance, becoming the most important tool in a brand's marketing arsenal. Where advertising focuses on promoting a brand, PR will play a crucial role in upholding credibility and authenticity. In this way, PR will provide a fillip to advertising as well. PR will likely guide communication strategies in the future, ensuring that the messaging is consistently aligned with the brand's values.

To conclude, the PR function is going to expand and evolve rapidly. The business ecosystem will bear witness to its massive shift as PR becomes more prominent and influential—a multifaceted, data-driven, indispensable core business function.

6

Dilip Cherian

Co-Founder of Perfect Relations, currently a crisis and communications strategy consultant

'I have a philosophy in life: if you're very good at something and can do it on autopilot, it's time to stop and try something new because you're no longer learning.'

From Economist to Journalist to Public Relations

I was born in a small village in Kerala called Niranam, my mother's hometown. Following tradition, my mother returned to her village for my birth. The place back then was connected only via the backwaters. Travelling to my grandparents' house involved first taking a cab, then getting on a boat with all our luggage—a cumbersome but adventurous journey. My father was working in Calcutta at the time, and as the first child, I lived in Niranam with my mother. I have two siblings: a brother who is now a doctor in the US and a sister who has spent her life teaching in England.

I was privileged to have been born in a tiny village and shortly thereafter transitioned to the big city—Calcutta. I grew up in Calcutta, where I attended school and college, living a typically middle-class urban life. My school was within walking distance of my home, and college was just a bus ride away. Education was highly valued in our family, and I was fortunate to attend one of the best schools. I managed to avoid the traditional IIT rat race by simply not taking the entrance exam, fearing I might actually pass.

I studied at Presidency College, then considered the best in India for economics. Having no prior exposure to the subject, I found it more engaging than accounting, which many of my peers pursued. I did briefly consider chartered accountancy, but soon realised that I couldn't distinguish between debits and credits, leading me to abandon that path.

My college years were intellectually stimulating. Presidency College was a hub of intellectual excitement and had historical links to the Naxalite movement. Some seniors had even been imprisoned and would sometimes carry guns on campus. I led student protests and organised the first non-political, purely cultural intercollegiate festival, establishing my knack for large-scale event management.

Although Bengali was not my first language, I learnt it in college. I had studied science in school under the Senior Cambridge exam system, which preceded the CBSE and ICSE. After college, I considered pursuing a master's degree in Calcutta but decided to apply to the Delhi School of Economics, influenced by a cousin who was studying there.

I completed my master's degree at the Delhi School of Economics and was advised by Professor Dharma Kumar to take up a job immediately. Her husband, the chairman of the Bureau of Industrial Costs and Prices (now the Tariff

Commission), facilitated my entry into the government as an economic consultant. After about two years, a former colleague invited me to join a new business magazine, *Business India*, in Bombay, marking the start of my journalism career, which lasted many years. When I joined *Business India*, I had a secretary from day one because I was not adept at typing, which my colleagues found quite amusing. However, the cost was deducted from my salary, which was less amusing, given that my salary was only about ₹1,000.

I quit when I realised I was doing six cover stories in six months for a fortnightly magazine, meaning I was responsible for every alternate cover story. I have a philosophy in life: if you're very good at something and can do it on autopilot, it's time to stop and do something else because you're no longer learning. When I noticed that I could handle cover stories with ease, something meant to be stressful and a significant achievement, I knew it was time to move on.

During my tenure, I had become the assistant deputy editor. Our editor fell ill, and I stepped in as the acting editor for two years while living in Bombay, despite being from Delhi. I had also started writing the first column on bureaucracy for any magazine or newspaper in India. *Business India* was a groundbreaking publication as it was the first business magazine, founded by Ashok Advani, who aimed to highlight positive news about business and businesspersons, contrasting with existing business newspapers like *The Economic Times* and *The Financial Express*.

Eventually, Dhirubhai Ambani invited me to join him in starting a newspaper. When I informed Ashok Advani, he questioned my decision, pointing out that I was already at the top. Nonetheless, I moved on to work with Dhirubhai

Ambani as the business editor for two years, collaborating closely with him, Mukesh and Anil Ambani, along with a diverse team. We set up a technologically advanced and well-designed newspaper, acquiring existing ones to avoid the hassle of obtaining new licenses, a move characteristic of Dhirubhai Ambani's strategic thinking.

After two years of preparation and one year of running the newspaper, I decided to quit. I had mastered the role and was ready for new ventures. I started several initiatives, including a restaurant called A Touch of Glass, a children's newspaper named Enjoy, and a design company called Fourth Quadrant. The latter was established as a start-up by five very bright young design engineers who had just graduated from IIT Delhi. One of our first major projects was designing a two-wheeler for a very large automotive company. Interestingly, the company is still around, but at the time, they had some strange and rather bizarre requirements for the project.

I attempted to launch a public policy magazine for MPs, MLAs and ministers, but the project didn't take off when the funding disappeared. In response, I decided to fill a market gap by starting an Indian-owned and -operated PR company. I co-founded Perfect Relations, with the acronym PR. My colleague Bobby Kewalramani joined me in this new venture. I had rented the drawing room of Shibu Soren, a tribal party leader, as an office space for the public policy magazine project, and we continued to work from there as we transitioned to Perfect Relations.

Our office was about half a kilometre from Rashtrapati Bhavan. I would draft press releases, and Bobby and I would hop on my motorcycle and ride to a public phone booth to call the media. After making the calls, we would return to the office, make photocopies of the press releases and then head to ITO on Bahadur Shah Zafar Marg, about 2.5 km away, to distribute them to various media offices, including PTI. This was the humble beginning of Perfect Relations: two men, a motorcycle, a telephone booth and a cyclostyle machine that wasn't even ours.

We were fortunate because an old schoolmate from Calcutta, who was the India CEO of PepsiCo, needed a new PR firm to work with as he wanted to change the incumbent PR firm. One day, he told me he wanted a reliable consultancy that understood his needs and offered a fixed monthly cost. I proposed a simple arrangement: we would agree on a fixed fee, billed three months in advance. If, after six months, either party felt the fee needed adjustment, we would negotiate accordingly.

This fixed-fee model became a benchmark for Perfect Relations and eventually influenced other companies. Our straightforward approach meant we didn't need an accountant initially; we simply sent an invoice, and they deposited the money. It wasn't until a year later that Royson joined us as our accountant.

As we grew and needed more people and space, we moved to various locations, marking the beginning of Perfect Relations' journey.

Most PR firms were affiliated with global consultancies, but I didn't want Perfect Relations to be just an add-on to a foreign firm. Our tagline was 'The Science of Image Management', a concept I created. I believed that managing an image was indeed a science, requiring us to work directly with the top executives, or what are now called the CXOs.

I insisted that unless we were working with the owner or chairman of the company, we weren't truly engaging with them. We didn't want to be a mere extension of the marketing department. Instead, we aimed to be seen as communication scientists reporting directly to the board. Our design was to avoid being tagged onto the advertising billing of the company and instead be integral to the strategic communication thinking of the board.

When Ramesh Vangal, our first client, mentioned that HTA was his advertising agency, I responded, 'That's your problem. We don't work through advertising agencies; we work directly with you.' I explained that we would create communication campaigns for all product launches, but they would be communication-driven, not advertising-driven. This was a new approach at the time, as everyone relied heavily on ad agencies.

Building our client base was slow work, with clients coming in one by one. However, we weren't in a hurry, as our bills were covered and our overheads were very low.

Two factors helped us gain business. First, my rapport with people at the ownership level of companies meant that I could understand their strategies and policies. I didn't want to create a company that merely translated instructions into action. Instead, I envisioned a consultancy that was part of the planning process, aiming to achieve the company's end objectives rather than just following their prescribed processes. This represented a significant mental shift for our clients.

I designed the PR firm to function more like a consulting practice than a traditional marketing firm. While it was marketing and consumer-led, it was also policy-oriented and highly strategic. Our approach focused on providing and receiving valuable inputs at the highest level, as we were dealing directly with the CEOs.

From a Foundational Role to Centre Stage

Essentially, the evolution of PR can be divided into two or three distinct phases. Phase I, which I consider the foundation for growth, began post-1991 with liberalisation. This period marked the first time the government and the establishment signalled that growth was positive. The profession was celebrated, corporates and capitalists became acceptable, and profit was acknowledged as something taxable but no longer viewed as a dirty word.

It also had two other significant implications. First, protectionism was going to decrease, exposing Indian companies to global influences and pressures. While it wasn't full-scale globalisation yet—that would come in a few years—the process had begun. During this phase, many companies recognised that PR would be essential as a tool for their business growth.

They recognised that without gaining visibility for their products and services, they would be unable to compete effectively. As licensing ended and global companies entered the market, competition intensified. Many companies believed that PR was their most powerful tool to ensure their products were visible, perceived as superior and seen as significant or dominant in the market. Unlike today's FOMO-driven excitement around start-ups, customers at that time prioritised reliability, visibility and guarantees. PR played a crucial role in meeting these customer expectations.

The early PR movers were those who recognised the market's shift. Previously, most PR firms were merely extensions of advertising agencies, offering perfunctory PR services primarily because clients requested them. These services were often provided as add-ons, sometimes even unpaid, to retain lucrative advertising budgets. Consequently, many PR companies at the time were essentially brand extensions or non-brand extensions of advertising agencies.

We established Perfect Relations during this period of change. We recognised the transformative moment unfolding. Having been a business journalist and an economist with the government, I understood that the market was evolving. Global companies were entering India, and they understood the value of PR. I also knew that the only place where you could influence thinking and communication strategy was in the boardroom. Therefore, I decided not to work with CMOs or PR managers—if I wasn't part of the boardroom, I wasn't interested in representing the company. This approach was risky, but it was based on providing a service that involved thinking outside the box and integrating communications into corporate strategy.

An Unfolding Journey

In my view, the future of PR is still unfolding. We can expect new possibilities and significant changes to emerge as we navigate three major factors. These factors are the hyperlocalisation of media, the disintermediation enabled by social media for CEOs and founders, and the disruptive impact of AI-driven creative tools. These trends are pivotal, and I will describe each one in detail below.

First, the consumer, policymaker, judge, decision-maker, rival CEO, potential employee, shareholder, analyst, bureaucrat, GST collector and factory inspector all represent the target audience that any communication programme will ultimately address. These diverse stakeholders are crucial to consider in any PR strategy.

The main idea is to understand what captures their attention, and most of the time, it's social media. Additionally, communication today often happens via WhatsApp and other digital media platforms. These methods share a common factor: they are accessed through handheld devices, primarily smartphones. Beyond these, there are other forms of media such as television, newspapers, magazines, radio, cinema and events.

In the attention-scarce economy we're entering, people are likely to browse content on their handheld devices. While they may be exposed to other media, their attention will frequently return to the small screen in front of them. This results in minimal and fragmented attention. These factors will significantly impact the PR practices in the future.

I'll give you a recent example with a trigger warning for sexual assault/harassment. A woman complained about being groped on a flight by an executive of a company. She tweeted about it to the chairman of the company. I messaged the chairman of the company, asking if he had seen the tweet. He responded that he had already apologised on X (formerly Twitter) and announced that action would be taken immediately.

This brings me to my second point: today, a CEO has a device that allows them to jump into the communication process directly, bypassing the lawyer, the broker, the PR advisor and the corporate strategist. The CEO's response on X was perfunctory, primary and minimal, yet he believed it was sufficient. In my opinion, it was not enough.

This example illustrates how PR has changed. A senior advisor reaches out to the chairman or founder about a problem on social media with legal, stock market and regulatory implications. The CEO decides to address all of these issues within ten minutes by sending a direct message himself, adding a layer of authenticity to the response. Although the message may incorporate parts of a draft provided to him and is curated to fit the medium, it is definitely in his own language. However, it lacks empathy, robustness and adequacy for the situation. This highlights the CEO's ability to respond directly and the tendency of many CEOs, who have received perfunctory training, to believe they can handle PR and its fallouts themselves.

The final aspect to consider is the role of AI. Could AI have helped the CEO crowdsource examples of how other owners or founders apologised when an employee was caught on the wrong side of the law? Yes. Could AI have provided ample material, drafted responses and revised them? Absolutely. In essence, much of the content creation, research and revision traditionally handled by consultancies and experts is increasingly being taken over by various AI tools.

In the next five years, we will likely see the number of top-level CEOs who are unaware of or do not use these tools diminish. This raises a crucial question: what will the role of PR be in such a landscape? That is the question that stays alive today.

7

Rajiv Desai

Founder of Indian Public Affairs Network (IPAN), currently Chairman, Comma Consulting

'PR during that time was a war against monopolies, both private and government-controlled. We supported new businesses entering India in the early 1990s, helping them navigate and succeed in a challenging environment.'

From Engineering to Journalism to Public Relations

I was born in 1949 in Surat, Gujarat, and was raised in Bombay. My grandfather was a medical practitioner and my parents government officers. I attended St Xavier's High School and Jai Hind College. Later, I studied mechanical engineering at MS University of Baroda.

A year or two into university, I was named to the editorial board of the college newspaper, *Emester*. During this time, I wrote an article—'Us Angry Young Men'—about a growing revolutionary fervour among students. It caught the attention of the Baroda correspondent of the newly founded Ahmedabad edition of *The Times of India*. He wrote about it. The story caught the attention of the resident editor, who chose to feature it on the front page, and soon after, I was invited to meet him at his office in Ahmedabad, some 100 km north. He offered me a job: writing a column and reporting 'spot news' from the MS University campus.

This opened for me a whole new world: from engineering to journalism. But try as I might, there was no way for me to transfer to the university's baccalaureate programme in Arts. That's when I decided to look at American universities for a graduate programme in journalism.

The Scripps Howard School of Journalism offered one of the best master's degree programmes. I applied and was selected. In September 1973, I found myself on an Air India flight headed to New York.

Landing at John Fitzgerald Kennedy Airport (JFK), I tried to reconcile the image in my mind with what was before me. I saw determined, friendly people in a hurry heading off to work, others going off on vacation or to join their families … out there in the vastness of America. But they found the time to nod and say hello. The reality was quite different from the image my mind had conjured.

The experience of graduate school was immensely satisfying. I made friends, many of whom I remained in touch with for many years after. It was the same with friends I made while pursuing a second master's degree.

Later, I moved to Chicago, where I joined a firm specialising in industrial advertising. Struck by my engineering background and writing skills, the company offered me a position as a copywriter. I took the job and bade farewell to the possibility of an academic career of teaching and research in political science.

My career in the communications business began with this specialist agency. The focus was on promoting machine tools, cutting tools and industrial automation systems. After a few years there, I joined the trade and technical unit of Hill and Knowlton, the world's largest PR consulting firm at that time. This experience eventually provided an opportunity to return to India and establish the country's first PR firm, IPAN (Indian Public Affairs Network) in 1987. This firm was part of the J. Walter Thompson (JWT) company in India, which was helmed by Hindustan Thompson Associates (HTA), India's premiere ad agency, and the market research firm IMRB.

I had never worked in India and had been away for so long that I was glad for the connection with HTA. It was a great start. IPAN was essentially my own firm and the management at HTA assured me that it would remain independent while being a part of the Thompson network.

It was crucial to establish that our PR firm was not part of the ad agency's media department, which hitherto distributed news releases and made placements in the media. This was to avoid the impression that IPAN would handle PR for HTA clients. Thus, from the outset, we maintained our independence and had our own clients, rarely taking on the ad agency's clients.

Back then, the landscape was different. Media buyers and ad agencies handled press releases, often overlooking the strategic potential of PR. We recognised this gap and introduced a new perspective. We offered PR counsel and services not just as a tactical tool but as a vital management strategy. This shift in mindset was groundbreaking, and we pioneered the idea of using PR to shape and manage public perceptions of companies, products and people, setting a new standard in the profession.

We adopted a unique approach that surprised many journalists. When asked about the principles guiding our PR company, I said it was based on 'Satyagraha', or the insistence on truth. This applied not only to our clients but also to the journalists we worked with. This approach was innovative and effective in the media industry where PR was often seen as simply killing a story or offering perks to news editors to get a story placed. Our commitment to ethical, proof-based PR set us apart and contributed significantly to our success.

Parallel to my career in communications, I also established a career in journalism. I wrote a column for the *Chicago Tribune* newspaper and founded a community newspaper, *India Tribune*, which continues to thrive. In India, I contributed to numerous newspapers and magazines, maintaining an active presence in the field of journalism.

I was very lucky with my first hires. They were straight out of college and essentially learnt everything about PR on the job. Although I had experience with PR in the US, India was a different landscape. We all learnt together and bonded on the job. The company took off like a rocket.

Working at IPAN was an absolute joy. Those years, from when I started to when I left, were the most exciting and enjoyable of my life. We organised off-sites, trips to various destinations, including places like Khajuraho, Mussoorie and more. It was a novel concept in India to take your staff on a retreat for several days, focusing on everything except work. We had a blast, and I've never had more fun anywhere else.

IPAN became known as the 'University of PR' because it attracted people from all backgrounds, mostly with no prior experience in PR. They joined, learnt, and many stayed with us for years. My senior team grew to include stalwarts from the profession and from journalism. They could hold their own against any competitor anywhere in the world. We stayed together for sixteen years, a tight-knit group, united by a clear vision of doing something different each time, not just repeating the same old routines. Additionally, we launched a parallel operation focusing on newspaper research and analysis, serving clients such as Rafale, the French aircraft manufacturer, a new player in the market. It was an exciting time indeed.

The 1990s were wonder years in India. To understand this, you had to be at Bombay's Oberoi Hotel on any weekday. Business leaders from the US, the UK, Continental Europe; from Singapore and Hong Kong; from Australia and New Zealand were there to establish a presence in the country.

As the pioneer in PR consulting, we were at the forefront of every new business venture entering India, whether it was in courier services, toiletries or even breakfast cereals like Kellogg's Cornflakes. Having worked in the US with the world's largest, most respected PR firm, I can say, with due modesty, I expected this to happen.

I can remember a conversation with an editor in Chicago, who was vociferously supportive of my plan to relocate to India. 'You're going to the right place at the right time,' he told me. 'Just think what American companies look for when they invest in a foreign country: legal support and PR counsel and services.'

IPAN's first client in India was a textile firm from Ahmedabad. They had just introduced new plans to manufacture denim in India. Other clients included firms seeking entry into the Indian market but who faced stiff opposition from local manufacturers, whose market share was threatened.

During this time, I learnt that PR wasn't just about formalities and polished presentations; it could also be a cutthroat game. The local competitors would plant negative stories about our client, which journalists readily published. When I confronted an editor about it, he said, 'You can always respond.' I argued that if the information was patently untrue, it should have been verified before publication. His response was, 'Then it wouldn't be a story.'

This experience revealed to me that much of journalism in India was handled by untrained individuals who prioritised controversy over accuracy. It was a stark contrast to my understanding of professional journalism.

That's how it all started. From our work with PepsiCo, we began to grow. PepsiCo faced significant challenges due to fierce domestic competition. Every time their file came up for approval, the All India Soft Drinks Manufacturers Association, primarily driven by a local brand, would stir up controversy on government priorities. This would cause the government to back off, saying they couldn't support PepsiCo.

We demonstrated that the issue wasn't about whether India needed Pepsi or the quality of Pepsi as a product. It was about breaking the monopoly held by one company in the soft drinks industry.

After successfully navigating this, we moved on to work with Citibank, continuing our growth and expanding our client base. Citibank wanted to launch their consumer services in India, which was a challenge, given the government-dominated financial sector. Citibank was perceived as a foreign bank catering to the wealthy and to multinationals. Their vision was to transform this by establishing branches, if not ATMs, in every neighbourhood, revolutionising retail banking in India. We were proud to assist in this transformation, focusing primarily on consumer services rather than merchant and investment banking.

Another significant client was Boeing, which was facing stiff competition from Airbus. The aircraft market was complex, and Boeing needed a strategic approach to navigate the challenges. We suggested they commission a comprehensive report on civil aviation in India, a ground-breaking PR effort that involved engaging with all stakeholders in the industry. This not only provided valuable insights but also paved the way for Boeing's success in the Indian market.

We also worked with the Express Industry Council of India, an association formed by courier firms, which were battling the postal department's monopoly on small parcel deliveries. The postal department threatened to shut down private courier services, but we fought back and won that battle, ensuring the survival and growth of the express industry.

It was an incredibly thrilling era, with a wave of new consumer products entering India, spanning from ice cream and soft drinks to denim and toiletries. As these innovations flooded the market, momentum grew exponentially. Our involvement with L'Oréal exemplified this period of growth. The Indian Soaps and Toiletries Manufacturers Association engaged us to advocate for reduced duties on cosmetics. High prices had hindered the cosmetics industry, driving consumers to purchase products abroad. By addressing these issues, they aimed to make cosmetics more accessible domestically. It was a time of unparalleled excitement, spanning from 1989 to the mid-2000s, particularly throughout the dynamic decade of the 1990s.

PR during that time was a war against monopolies, both private and government-controlled. We supported new businesses entering India in the early 1990s, helping them navigate and succeed in a challenging environment. Our offices in Delhi, Bombay, Calcutta and Madras were hubs of activity. It appeared that India was on the move, with companies striving to launch new products and establish new ventures.

It was an exciting and transformative period in India, and we were at the heart of it, enjoying every moment. PR was not just about glossing over issues and putting on a good face; it was a hard-fought battle to dismantle vested interests and allow the market to flourish. And that's exactly what happened.

A Long Hop to PR Consulting

'You kill the story and I'll get you two tickets on the Rajdhani.' That was pretty much a defining feature of the relationship between journalists and the PR department of major companies. From there to PR consulting was a long hop. I can remember when a senior bureaucrat in Delhi asked me, 'So, for which company are you doing PR?'

We drew up a list of firms who were launching new products or projects and decided to reach out to them. It was a tough sell to people used to advertising as a way of using media to sell products. Of course, contacts helped; an early client was a textile firm that was just about to launch a denim manufacturing unit.

Denim? In India? That's when I learnt about denim and its origins ... and that the 'dungaree' got its name from Dongri, the port town near Bombay.

Our campaign incorporated the city where the mill was located and was also home to the Gandhi Ashram. Projecting it as an innovation hub, we called our campaign 'From the charkha to the chimney'. It worked. We were up and running.

In our version of the practice, we always sought to link a campaign to a larger cause. For example, one of the campaigns for an international bank's consumer group was titled 'Satyagraha and Small Dreams'.

Since then, PR has become mainstream and its practice much less exalted, focused on news releases, media lists, events and promotions.

A New Approach for the Future

Led by the penetration of the internet, the number of available communications channels has increased in ways hitherto unforeseen. With the proliferation of laptops, computers and mobile phones, opportunities for message delivery have increased exponentially.

Years ago, in a keynote speech, I made the point that the increase in media would have an inverse relationship with comprehension and calls to action. Today, you have the equivalent of a split-second opportunity to be heard.

That calls for an entirely new approach to media and messages.

8

Sunil Gautam

Founder of Clea Advertising, Clea Public Relations and Hanmer & Partners, currently Founder and Partner, Pitchfork Partners

'Empowering people, something I learnt early on, is crucial. By empowering them, you foster resilience. This attracts good people who are willing to shoulder responsibilities.'

From Investment Banking to Public Relations

My father, a principled man in government service, valued education above all for his four children. I am the youngest, with three highly educated siblings. We lived in Mumbai, and I attended New Era School. While my siblings pursued science and went abroad, I chose to study commerce at Siddharth College.

After graduation, I joined the firm G.P. Kapadia for my chartered accountancy (CA) articleship and completed my CA, but realised it wasn't my passion. I aspired to become a banker. In 1979, I targeted American banks and landed a position at American Express, only to find that I was unhappy in back-end accounting.

At twenty-five, seeking a change, I joined Pressman Advertising. My career spanned several fields: CA firms, investment banking and finally advertising. Initially unsure, I grew to enjoy advertising, particularly account planning and client servicing. Despite enjoying three years in advertising, I eventually left and returned to my CA practice.

At twenty-nine, while practising as a CA, a friend encouraged me to start my own advertising agency. Despite limited resources, I decided to try. My friend introduced me to a potential client, and we worked hard, winning the Essar account. We launched Clea Advertising in 1985, quickly becoming the top agency in our field for seven consecutive years. Interestingly, Clea is my partner P. Venugopal's daughter's name. When she was born, he was reading a book that had a character named Clea, and he decided to name his daughter after that character. When we were looking for a name for our company, he suggested 'Clea', thinking it sounded beautiful. We knew we couldn't find anything better than that.

We expanded by creating Clea Investor Support Services, conducting daily IPO market research in a hundred cities, and launched a finance-focused magazine, *Above Par*. In 1995, we established Clea PR with a CEO brought in from an external organisation.

I left Clea on 30 June 1999 and launched Hanmer & Partners on 28 July 1999. We affiliated with MSL for global PR practices and access to international clients, eventually selling the company to Publicis Groupe in 2007. I stepped down in 2011, passing the baton to my friend and colleague Jaideep

Shergill, who became the CEO. I remained as the executive chairman for four more years. Pitchfork was founded in 2015.

Also, when deciding on a name for my firm, I wanted it to convey seriousness, akin to a respected law firm. We examined various names at that time. Globally, PR consultancies often use individual names. With the guidance of a dear friend, we settled on Hanmer & Partners, aiming for a strong, professional impression.

The first client I signed, just a day before launching the firm, was an old advertising client who transitioned into becoming a PR client—Global Telesystems. Among the initial ten clients, we also had EY and the Bombay Stock Exchange.

Creating a strong reputation was crucial for us. When we started Hanmer & Partners, advertising agency peers offered us their properties for rent, which made us proud. Despite financial constraints, we placed a large recruitment ad in the newspaper, receiving numerous applications in 2000–01, amidst the dot-com boom. Our aim was to meet as many candidates as possible to ensure they became our ambassadors, interviewing over 500 people. Every weekend we would sit down for interviews. Rather than bombarding candidates with questions, we focused on explaining what Hanmer stood for and our vision for the future. As for the number we hired at that time, I don't recall the exact figure, but we were one of the largest in terms of staff. By 2006–07, we had around 350–400 people.

A Dynamic Dance of Society and Technology

From the era of press releases to crafting a strategic symphony of storytelling in a digitally driven world, the evolution of PR over two decades mirrors the dynamic dance of society and technology. Having witnessed the evolution firsthand, I can attest to the significant shifts that have reshaped the landscape of our profession, starting with the advent of digital technology. With the rise of the internet, social media platforms and digital tools, the dissemination of information has become instantaneous and ubiquitous. This has had a profound impact on PR practices, necessitating a more agile and adaptive approach to engagement.

Before digital dominance, press releases and print placements reigned supreme. Today, however, the field has evolved into a more strategy-driven discipline not relegated to merely media interactions. I like the fact that our field has increasingly become more professional, and the communication has become more nuanced and complex, shifting from being tactical to strategic. At its core, PR remains about building relationships and managing reputations. However, the methods and tools we employ for captivating audiences have intertwined with the ever-changing media landscape. Technology, as always, has made us constantly update our tactics and discover new ones that help us meet our communication goals. This dynamic nature of society, technology and business environment is a plus for the PR profession because it underscores the importance of strategic communication now more than ever. This was made evident in a recent survey by PRCAI, where it was found that India Inc. is allocating a much higher percentage of its marketing budget to PR than earlier.[*]

---

* 'SPRINT: Study of Public Relations Insights, Nuggets and Trends 2022-23', *Public Relations Consultants Association of India*, https://prcai.org/cms/images/pdf/SPRINT_Report_23_PRCAI.pdf.

I also want to stress on the globalisation of markets and how that has expanded the scope and complexity of PR initiatives. As companies operate in increasingly diverse and interconnected environments, PR strategies must account for cultural nuances, regulatory frameworks and geopolitical dynamics. This requires PR professionals to possess not only a deep understanding of local contexts but also a global perspective that enables them to navigate cross-cultural communication challenges.

As I mentioned earlier, strategy has taken centre stage, and the entire communication process has become more proactive than its earlier, reactionary avatar. PR professionals are no longer relegated to merely sending press releases and getting mentions in the media. We must now play a central role in shaping organisational reputation, driving stakeholder engagement and contribute to business objectives. This strategic alignment requires us to collaborate closely with leadership teams, integrate PR into broader marketing and communications strategies, and demonstrate tangible outcomes that align with organisational goals.

There has been a seminal difference in the way we measure outcomes as well. Gone are the days of relying solely on output metrics such as media impressions; today's PR professionals must demonstrate tangible outcomes and return on investment. From sentiment analysis and media monitoring to web analytics and stakeholder surveys, there are so many useful tools and methodologies available to assess the impact and effectiveness of PR campaigns.

The world of PR is in a constant state of flux, and success in the years to come will largely depend on one's ability to adapt to new technology and effectively communicate with audiences across age groups. The future may see an influx of technology for all PR professionals, but the essence of storytelling will always remain. The methods and tools may evolve, but the power of compelling narratives will endure.

An Exciting and Challenging Future Ahead

The future of the PR business holds both exciting opportunities and significant challenges owing to the multitude of factors I mentioned earlier—namely, technological advancements, changing consumer behaviours and evolving media landscapes. To start with, the continued proliferation of digital technology will continue to dominate how PR practitioners engage with audiences. From artificial intelligence to big data analytics, and even AR and VR, PR professionals must embrace emerging technologies and leverage them to offer new avenues for content creation and audience engagement.

Something we have not touched upon yet, and a lot of people often overlook, is the rise of stakeholder capitalism. The proliferation of digital technology has driven consumers to demand greater transparency and accountability from brands. Purpose-driven communication today holds more meaning than it ever has in our field. I would advise PR professionals to prioritise ethical considerations, sustainability initiatives and social impact storytelling in their communications strategies. In our era of heightened social consciousness and activism, building trust and maintaining it are of utmost importance.

Today, we are witnessing an unprecedented rate of democratisation of the media. User-generated content has emboldened both individuals and communities to influence public discourse, and brands are well aware of this. PR professionals must use this opportunity to engage with influencers and advocates and build meaningful relationships with them, as this opens an entirely new avenue of communication on behalf of our clients. In the face of a decentralised media landscape, our relationships with influencers and advocates have become a very useful tool.

The future of the PR business holds immense promise for those willing to embrace change, innovate and adapt to emerging trends. By harnessing the power of technology, embracing integration, prioritising purpose-driven communication and building meaningful relationships with influencers and advocates, PR professionals can position themselves as trusted advisors and strategic partners in shaping the narratives of tomorrow.

9

Aman Gupta

Co-Founder of SPAG, currently Managing Partner, SPAG FINN Partners

'We are proud of our role as a communications consultancy that acts as a strategic advisor and thought leader in this space.'

From Pharmaceutical Marketing to Public Relations

I was born in New Delhi, where my father worked with the Ministry of Home Affairs for the Government of India. I completed my schooling at Dev Samaj Modern School and Apeejay School, focusing on science in junior college, influenced by my brother who was pursuing his education from IIT. Following in his footsteps, I cleared the IIT JEE and began my engineering studies at IIT-BHU Varanasi, graduating in 1994.

We were a typical Indian middle-class family, where we were expected to become either engineers or doctors. Our parents couldn't afford to pay donations for college admissions, so it was drilled into us that excelling academically was the way to build a successful future. Coming from a service-oriented background, I was the first in my family to venture into business. Starting a business was never really considered an option when I was growing up.

So, after graduation, I started my career as a management trainee at Ranbaxy, where I spent two years in sales and marketing. This experience provided valuable insights into the ground realities of India. Subsequently, I decided to pursue an MBA and joined IMI in Qutab Institutional Area for a two-year post-graduation in marketing. It was there that I was introduced to PR by Dilip Cherian, who taught us the subject.

After completing my MBA, I moved to Mumbai and worked as a brand manager at Lupin, a pharmaceutical company. These roles deepened my involvement in the pharma and healthcare sectors. In 2000, I decided to return to Delhi and left my job in Mumbai. While searching for new opportunities, I received a call from Perfect Relations. They were looking for someone with a healthcare background, so I attended an interview. Coincidentally, the HR person was my neighbour.

PR was not initially on my radar, as I had a strong background in marketing. However, while looking for a job in marketing, I decided to take up this opportunity. At that time, Perfect Relations was setting up Imprimis PR as a separate entity for healthcare and pharma. I joined as a senior executive on 27 January 2000, under the guidance of CEO Bhuvnesh Chawla. Two months later, Bhuvnesh resigned, and I was left without a boss, leading to my unexpected promotion to CEO. I often share this story to illustrate that rapid growth is possible in our profession, as I went from a senior executive to CEO in just two months. From there until 2014, as CEO, I built the organisation into one of the largest healthcare communications consultancies. It was a tremendous learning curve, as I got the opportunity to work with some of the biggest global names, both companies and individuals. This included managing relations with Bill and Melinda Gates for the Gates Foundation, working with Richard Gere for his foundation and engaging with Queen Rania of Jordan, along with some of the largest pharmaceutical and healthcare companies.

By 2014, I decided it was time to move on and start my own venture. Shivani was already running the platform 'PR in India' at the time, focusing on lifestyle and luxury. They were also the go-to company for other PR firms looking to tap into a network of stringers. The model was different from traditional PR firms. After leaving my previous role, I was determined not to go back into a conventional job. So, I collaborated with Shivani. Given my background in healthcare, we decided to pivot the focus towards health. We acquired a few significant clients and rebranded the firm as SPAG. It's been ten years since then, and we have continued to grow and evolve in the healthcare communications sector.

The SPAG journey has been amazing, though not entirely what we had initially envisioned. We weren't sure how we would achieve our goals, but things fell into place as we went along. From securing some of the biggest clients early on to becoming one of the most awarded firms, our progress has been remarkable. We started in 2014, and by 2015, we were named the Global New PR Consultancy of the Year by PRovoke/Holmes Report. We remain the only firm from Asia to achieve this recognition, reflecting our rapid growth.

We always aimed to be the first Indian firm with a footprint outside India, leading to the establishment of our Singapore office in 2016. Many considered it a bold and perhaps foolish move, given the financial challenges of earning in Indian rupees and spending in US dollars. Our initial attempt wasn't successful; after two years of significant investment, we had to pause and reassess our strategy. However, we re-entered the market in 2018–19, and since then, our Southeast Asia operations have grown significantly, now contributing 35–40 per cent of our revenue. We remain one of the few firms with a full-fledged presence in the Asian region.

To enhance our capabilities, we acquired a company called Giga Health to expand our medical communications expertise. Additionally, we launched a separate digital firm called D Yellow Elephant, becoming pioneers in the digital pharma space. This gave us a significant first-mover advantage.

We are proud of our role as a communications consultancy that acts as a strategic advisor and thought leader in this space. Over our ten-year journey, we have produced a remarkable amount of thought leadership and research studies, likely unmatched by many globally. From our Digital Health Report in 2015 and 2017 to our Asia Pacific Report on healthcare communications with KPMG, we have consistently set the standard. We have developed tools like VET and collaborated with Great Place to Work to explore the future of the workforce and empower our staff. Our work on the start-up ecosystem is another example of our significant contributions. These thought leadership pieces, created in collaboration with top organisations like KPMG and Great Place to Work, have positioned SPAG as the go-to organisation in the healthcare communications sector. We have remained focused on this sector with a presence across Asia, making our journey unique and impactful.

When we were acquired by FINN Partners, we entered the next stage of growth. Now, as part of a global network, our work spans Asia Pacific, the Middle East and Africa. This collaboration has been excellent, as we share similar cultural values and a focus on health, aligning well with our original working philosophies.

From the beginning, we believed that success is not about the size or number of people but the quality of the people we have. We have stayed true to this principle. The same applies to our clients—it's not about quantity, but about working with clients who believe in our mission, the power of communication and advocacy. These clients are willing to invest in and respect our work. Our growth is a testament to this philosophy. It's about year-on-year growth driven by delivering business impact, building relationships and maintaining a reputation as a thought leader in the space. We have always aimed to have fun while growing, staying true to our core values and commitment to excellence.

As a public health expert, I understand the global challenges in making the world a healthier place. The role we play in public health communication is incredibly enriching. By harnessing the power of communication, we can encourage people to seek the right treatments and early diagnoses that can transform their lives. For instance, we have inspired individuals to get diagnosed and receive treatment for health issues they were unaware of, dramatically changing their lives for the better.

This is the true power of communication. Despite scepticism about the role of PR, the work we do significantly contributes to a healthier world. During the COVID-19 pandemic, we worked closely with the World Health Organization to tackle misinformation and control rumours, addressing critical issues on a global scale. Our efforts go beyond business and revenue, they are about delivering impact and having a purpose in making the world a better place.

Ritika Jauhari was with Shivani when I started SPAG, and Siddharth Kashyap, who joined me from Imprimis, strongly believed in our vision. Aditi Roy, passionate about health, played a key role in our growth and is now with Novartis. Chandni Dalal is now in Europe. These individuals were crucial during the early stages of our growth. Many others contributed at various stages, even if only for a short time, and their contributions were significant in building SPAG into what it is today.

My first client was a company called PHRMA, an association of all the pharmacies. They were my clients during my days at Imprimis and wanted to continue working with me when I moved. Another significant client was the Global Innovation Policy Center (GIPC). ADVAMED, an association of medical devices companies, was also one of our major clients. These were our first three significant clients when we started off.

The campaign for the Global Innovation Center, which continues to be a client, focuses on the value of innovation. It has received numerous awards and remains one of the longest-running campaigns in intellectual property (IP). The Annual Report, known as the Index, has significantly influenced IP policies not only in India but also globally. Starting as a client in India, we now collaborate with them across multiple geographies. This client holds significant importance for us and is one I am proud to highlight.

Merging PR, Marketing and Advertising

The PR profession has undergone a significant transformation in the last two decades, wherein it has evolved from a tool that was seen from a peripheral vision to being considered at the centre of business strategy. We can divide the last two decades into the following phases.

Traditional dominance (early 2000s): In the early 2000s, traditional media channels such as print, radio and television dominated the PR landscape. The primary tools of the trade included press releases, media kits and face-to-face interactions with journalists. PR professionals relied heavily on their relationships with media gatekeepers to secure coverage. The focus was on controlling the message and ensuring it reached the audience through trusted third parties.

Digital emergence (mid-to-late 2000s): This period saw the advent of digital media, which began to reshape the PR profession. The rise of the internet and the proliferation of online news outlets created new opportunities and challenges. PR professionals started incorporating online strategies, including email campaigns and digital press releases. Social media platforms such as Facebook, X (earlier Twitter) and LinkedIn emerged, offering new avenues for direct engagement with audiences. The role of PR began to shift from solely managing media relations to also covering digital content creation and distribution. Measuring the impact of PR efforts through web analytics became increasingly important, enabling more data-driven decision-making.

Social media revolution (2010s): The 2010s marked the social media revolution, fundamentally changing the PR landscape. Social media platforms became essential tools for PR professionals, enabling direct consumer interaction and real-time communication. This period saw the rise of influencer marketing, where individuals with large social media followings became critical players in shaping public opinion. Content creation diversified, with video, infographics and interactive content becoming central to PR strategies. The immediacy of social media also meant that crisis management had to evolve, with organisations needing to respond swiftly and transparently to any negative incidents.

Integrated communications (late 2010s to early 2020s): As the 2010s drew to a close, the lines between PR, marketing and advertising began to blur, leading to an era of integrated communications. PR professionals needed to collaborate more closely with other departments to create cohesive and comprehensive communication strategies. The emphasis shifted towards storytelling and building authentic relationships with audiences. This phase also saw the rise of data analytics and artificial intelligence in PR. Advanced tools allowed more precise targeting and measurement of PR efforts, making it possible to tailor messages to specific audiences and track their impact more accurately.

The era of purpose and authenticity (2020s): A heightened focus on purpose and authenticity characterises the current phase. Consumers increasingly expect brands to take a stand on social issues and demonstrate a genuine commitment to ethical practices. PR has become a critical function in managing corporate social responsibility (CSR) and sustainability initiatives. The COVID-19 pandemic accelerated the need for transparent and empathetic communication. PR professionals are now tasked with promoting products and services, fostering trust and demonstrating corporate values. The role of PR has expanded to include internal communications, as employee engagement and morale have become vital components of organisational success.

Looking into the Crystal Ball

When we look into the crystal ball, we see several emerging trends poised to shape the future of PR. As we navigate an increasingly complex and interconnected world, PR professionals must stay ahead of these trends to remain relevant and practical.

Hyper-personalisation and data-driven insights: Clients are seeking measurable impact for every rupee they spend, and the same is being asked of PR leaders. Therefore, the future of PR will be heavily influenced by the ability to leverage data analytics, which can show impact by audience engagement, behaviour impact and connectedness to business goals. Hyper-personalisation, where messages are tailored to individual preferences and behaviours, will become the norm. Advanced analytics will enable PR professionals to predict trends, understand audience sentiment in real time and measure the effectiveness of their campaigns with unprecedented precision. This data-driven approach will allow more targeted and impactful communication strategies.

Ethical communication and era of purpose to continue: The emphasis on ethical communication and purpose as core to organisation positioning will continue to grow. Consumers are becoming increasingly conscious of the ethical implications of their choices and expect brands to act responsibly. PR professionals will need to ensure that their organisations communicate their purpose initiatives effectively and demonstrate genuine commitment to social and environmental causes. Transparency and authenticity will be key in building and maintaining trust with stakeholders.

Crisis management in a hyper-connected world: Effective crisis management will be more critical in an era in which information spreads rapidly across digital and social platforms. PR professionals will need to develop robust, agile and responsive crisis communication plans. Managing reputational risks and responding swiftly to crises will be essential. This includes monitoring social media in real time, engaging with stakeholders proactively and providing timely and accurate information to mitigate potential damage.

Continued integration of PR and marketing: The lines between PR and marketing will continue to blur, leading to further integration of these functions. PR professionals will increasingly collaborate with marketing teams to create unified communication strategies that leverage the strengths of both disciplines. This integration will enable more cohesive storytelling and brand messaging, ensuring a consistent and engaging audience experience across all touchpoints.

Evolving role of influencers: The role of influencers in PR will continue to evolve. While influencers will remain important, there will be a shift towards micro-influencers and nano-influencers who have smaller but highly engaged and loyal followings. Authenticity and credibility will be the essential criteria for selecting influencers as audiences become more discerning about the endorsements they trust. Long-term partnerships with influencers who align with the brand's values and ethos will be prioritised over one-off collaborations.

10

Shivani Gupta

Co-Founder of SPAG, currently Managing Partner, SPAG FINN Partners

'Patience and perseverance are essential to accomplish what you set out to do. Keep your goals in mind and work towards them consistently.'

Exploring the Uncharted Territory of Public Relations

I spent most of my childhood in Mumbai and Delhi, moving frequently because of my father's job at the bank. These cities played a significant role in my upbringing. I completed part of my schooling and my undergraduate education at Narsee Monjee College in Mumbai.

Thanks to my father's connections in the industry, we had the privilege of interacting with Bollywood stars, making our time there exciting.

Even though he came from a banking background, my father was known for his client-focused approach, going above and beyond to help them and thus earning their deep respect.

This ethos of compassion and selflessness has profoundly influenced my brother and me.

My father's dedication to helping others, like assisting people with opening bank accounts when they couldn't afford to, left a lasting impression on us. His generosity extended to giving away his own belongings to those in need. My mother, a simple person, also contributed to shaping our values.

After completing my undergraduate studies in Mumbai, I moved to Delhi with my family, as my father had been transferred. I pursued a master's in communication from the National Institute of Advertising. When I entered the communications sector, it was still a very new field. Not many people were pursuing the subject at that time. However, we had access to some of the leading professionals from various firms, including advertising and PR, who served as our professors.

I undertook internships at several places during my undergraduate course, including Clea PR. When the final placement interviews at the university took place, I was selected by Imprimis PR. Initially, I wasn't keen on joining a firm focused on the healthcare sector, as I found it quite serious and wasn't sure if it was the right fit for me. However, my placement coordinator emphasised the importance of Imprimis PR, noting it was a leading healthcare PR firm and part of Perfect Relations, the top PR consultancy at the time.

I decided to learn from the best and joined Imprimis PR. Working under Aman Gupta, who was the then CEO, I gained valuable experience. I learnt how Perfect Relations trains and develops its employees. I worked closely with different clients and team leaders, and eventually became involved in new business development and pitches.

During this time, Aman and I decided to get married. Company policy at Perfect Relations prevented us from working in the same organisation once engaged, so I had to leave. Fortunately, I received an opportunity from one of my clients, Becton Dickinson (BD). Initially, I worked with their division handling lab tubes, but soon, my work was recognised, and I was asked to handle multiple divisions.

At BD, I joined the senior leadership team led by CEO Ram Sharma. At the age of twenty-three, I found myself in the boardroom with senior business heads, working on a complete marketing revamp. This involved building websites and intranets and managing internal communications. It was a challenging and fast-paced environment, but I enjoyed it.

Despite being hired for one division, I ended up managing the entire branding and marketing efforts of the firm. I worked late hours, learning from IT teams about backend operations and website management, to ensure I could independently handle content updates. Ram Sharma's vision played a crucial role in my development.

Eventually, I got married and had my son, Pratham. I never stopped working, though I took a short break when I left BD. After my break, I joined AuthBridge, a background research company, where I headed the communications department and reported directly to the CEO. Once again, I found myself in a prominent role, significantly raising the company's media profile.

During my time at AuthBridge, I made a notable impact, getting the company featured in major publications. It was a proud moment for me and the team, seeing our work recognised and celebrated in the media.

Then, suddenly, my mother was diagnosed with a very rare form of cancer that had no cure in India, and there were very few doctors globally who could treat it. This news was devastating and completely shattered us. It was an extremely challenging time, but thankfully, my mother's condition improved, and she was cured within two months. During this period, my organisation, AuthBridge, was incredibly supportive and allowed me to work remotely and flexibly.

After this phase, I left AuthBridge and started 'PR in India', a consultancy network with a keen focus on the challenging media landscape, particularly in reaching remote areas where consultancy outreach was limited. As we handled media relations for numerous firms and corporates, I also started signing up my own clients, spanning the hospitality, travel, consumer goods, fashion and lifestyle sectors. We organised fashion shows involving celebrities, gradually expanding our client base. Ritika Jauhari later joined me, impressing me with her determination after a career break, becoming a pivotal team member. Hiring her remains one of my best decisions.

In 2014, Aman joined PR in India. Given his background and passion for health, the focus naturally shifted towards the healthcare sector. It wasn't an intentional change but happened organically. Aman's presence made rebranding inevitable. The focus of the company shifted entirely towards health. Aman had decided not to take any Imprimis clients for the next few years. Despite this, there were people who insisted on working with him wherever he went. Even with the insistence, we adhered to Aman's decision and did not take on those clients. Instead, we focused on advocacy projects and public affairs. Thus, we began our journey as a public affairs and advocacy firm, SPAG. SPAG was already a registered name—it stands for two things: Shivani Pratham Aman Gupta and also Strategic Partners Group.

We are dedicated to giving back to society and doing good for the world by spreading messages that might not reach the grassroots—informing people about cures and solutions they might not know exist. Creating awareness about numerous critical illnesses, from various diseases to the therapies and innovations available, is crucial. Most importantly, it's about bringing innovation closer to those who lack access, promoting health equity. Health equity means ensuring that everyone benefits, not just those with easy access to information, top doctors and advanced healthcare infrastructure. It involves reaching those who do not have access to these resources and ensuring they are informed and cared for.

We conducted several campaigns on heart failure and related topics. For instance, many people, including myself, didn't know the difference between a heart attack and heart failure until we began working on these campaigns and researching the subject. Our team felt immense pride in the campaigns we worked on. Even today, we share personal stories about how these campaigns made a difference in our lives. For example, one team member mentioned how she told her family about our campaign when a health issue arose. Her mother advised her to consult a doctor based on the information from our campaign, showcasing the real impact of our work.

Everything we do has a purpose. It's not just about creating content without meaning or acting like a manufacturing machine. Our focus is on strategic thinking rather than just producing high volumes of content. It's all about quality over quantity. We are not interested in simply generating numerous media clips. Instead, we prioritise the quality of our work, which is why we focus on quality while hiring people rather than simply increasing the number of staff. Our ambition is not measured by numbers but by the quality and impact of our work. We have always aimed to do good, award-winning work. In fact, we have often turned down projects that we felt were merely routine and didn't contribute positively to society. Before FINN Partners acquired us, we used to use the tagline 'Be Real', emphasising the genuine quality of our work. We believe in showing the true picture, not a coloured one. Also, creating intellectual property (IP) is something very close to my heart. I have a passion for developing IPs.

We have significantly diversified and grown our creative and digital teams. The campaigns we have worked on have been noteworthy. Ritika Jauhari has been a core part of SPAG, with a background in lifestyle and fashion PR before joining us. Today, she is considered a health PR guru with many years of experience.

Our partnership with FINN Partners began recently. Conversations started in 2020, and we found that our values and culture aligned with theirs. We met with their team, including Peter Finn—the founder—along with Gil Bashe and Howard Solomon. We were impressed by their brilliance and amazing personalities. Although we hadn't initially planned to take this step, we realised how similar our values and purpose-driven work were and decided to go ahead. Even now, we feel in control and valued as health issue experts in Asia. FINN Partners sought us out for our expertise in this region, and it's been a fantastic partnership, allowing us to share our best practices and collaborate effectively.

The best part is that we are able to leverage global intelligence, cutting-edge technology and innovation while having our own dedicated space to work in. Additionally, Peter often speaks about his father's values and culture, emphasising the importance of FINN Partners being personable and people oriented. (For those who are unaware, Peter Finn's father David Finn was the co-founder of the iconic firm Ruder Finn along with William Ruder.) This is why the firm's tagline is 'A company with a heart and conscience'. Their primary focus is on ensuring people are happy and doing purpose-driven work. They are committed to making an impact and a difference in the world through their work.

We are definitely moving towards expanding into different sectors, but healthcare will always be our first priority. Today, we proudly work with excellent tech clients, and we have already begun our ventures in the travel sector.

I love Adam Grant's books; he presents concepts that resonate deeply with me. He emphasises the importance of flexibility and agility in our actions and the need to adapt when change is required rather than being stubborn. People in any profession should be prepared to adapt and remain agile, especially in PR. The world is constantly evolving, with new technologies and innovations emerging every day. To keep up, it's important to continuously upskill yourself. If you think, 'This isn't my thing,' you will never be able to learn anything new. This applies to me and to anyone striving for growth. I think it's crucial for today's generation to learn not to feel overwhelmed or believe that they cannot achieve their goals. It's important not to give up too soon. Patience and perseverance are essential to accomplish what you set out to do. Keep your goals in mind and work towards them consistently.

Redefining PR as Essential Strategic Partners for Long-Term Success

The landscape of PR has undergone a profound transformation, driven by technological advancements, changing media dynamics and shifting consumer expectations. PR has evolved from a primarily reactive function into a proactive, strategic partner within organisations. Once siloed and focused on media relations and crisis management, it is now integral to broaden business strategies, working closely with leadership teams and playing a crucial role in the strategic boardroom. This evolution has redefined PR professionals as essential strategic partners in achieving long-term success.

The digital revolution has dramatically altered the PR landscape. While traditional media—print, TV and radio—dominated the space two decades ago, digital and social media platforms have revolutionised communication, allowing direct, real-time interaction with consumers and stakeholders. This shift has made PR more immediate, responsive and interactive. The advent of data analytics has further transformed PR from an art into a science. Today, sophisticated tools enable precise tracking and measurement of PR campaigns, providing data-driven insights for better decision-making and demonstrating clear ROI to stakeholders.

The proliferation of new media channels, including podcasts, blogs, vlogs and influencer partnerships, has broadened the scope of PR, offering unique storytelling and audience engagement opportunities. Effective use of these channels has become a critical skill for PR professionals. In an era of information overload and heightened scepticism, authenticity and transparency have become paramount. Unlike the polished, controlled messaging of the past, today's audiences demand honesty and genuine engagement, with successful PR campaigns focusing on building trust and credibility through transparent communication.

The integration of AI and machine learning into PR practices is a significant recent development, enhancing capabilities for media monitoring, sentiment analysis and predictive analytics. These tools allow PR professionals to anticipate trends, understand audience sentiments and tailor strategies with greater precision, leading to more effective campaigns. Finally, the concept of integrated campaigns has become central to contemporary PR, combining elements of influencer marketing, social media and digital strategies. This holistic approach ensures cohesive messaging across all touchpoints, maximising reach and impact. In today's competitive landscape, PR specialists are not just communicators but architects of reputation, growth drivers and catalysts for organisational success, playing a pivotal role in shaping public perception, driving brand loyalty and securing a competitive edge.

An Ever-Changing Landscape

The future of PR stands on the brink of transformative evolution, propelled by pivotal trends and technological advancements that promise to redefine its landscape and amplify its impact.

The role of PR has evolved far beyond traditional communication tactics, becoming a critical component of comprehensive business strategies. This shift necessitates that PR efforts align seamlessly with overarching business objectives, driving measurable outcomes that contribute to organisational success. By embedding PR within the business framework, we can elevate brand reputation, influence stakeholder perceptions and directly stimulate business growth. The future demands that PR actively enhances organisational achievements, becoming indispensable to strategic business operations.

The ever-changing media landscape requires PR professionals to adapt continually and innovate. While earned media remains fundamental, a diversified media mix is essential for future success. Digital platforms, social media, podcasts and influencer collaborations are increasingly pivotal. Clients now seek impactful and compelling narratives that resonate across multiple channels. Crafting stories that captivate audiences on diverse platforms will be crucial for maintaining relevance and driving engagement in an increasingly fragmented media environment.

In a world where digital interactions prevail, authenticity and human connection are paramount. Modern audiences value genuine, relatable interactions and can quickly detect insincerity. Therefore, PR campaigns must prioritise authentic, humanised communication to build trust and credibility. Focusing on real personal connections will foster deeper engagement with audiences, thereby enhancing the overall impact of PR initiatives.

AI is revolutionising PR, offering advanced capabilities for media monitoring, trend analysis and strategic decision-making. AI-driven insights allow us to identify emerging trends, gauge public sentiment and tailor strategies with unprecedented precision. To remain at the forefront, it is imperative to embrace these technological advancements, thereby enhancing the efficiency and effectiveness of PR campaigns.

The future of PR lies in the adoption of integrated campaigns that employ a comprehensive, 360-degree approach. PR no longer operates in isolation but works in tandem with other marketing and communication disciplines. This includes influencer marketing, social media and digital initiatives, ensuring cohesive messaging and broader reach. By adopting a holistic approach, PR professionals can meet the evolving demands of the profession and achieve maximum impact, ensuring that PR remains a vital, dynamic force in the business world.

The future of PR is marked by its critical integration into business strategy, the necessity for a diversified media approach, the importance of authenticity, the transformative power of AI and the adoption of integrated campaigns. These elements collectively herald a new era for PR, one characterised by enhanced impact, strategic alignment and a profound connection with audiences.

11

Vineet Handa

Founder and CEO of Kaizzen

'Fostering a culture of kindness and humanity is crucial. This applies not only to our external interactions but also to our internal stakeholders.'

Away from the Family Business into Media

I was born and raised in Chhindwara, a small town in Madhya Pradesh, which serves as the district headquarters. Our family was well-to-do and known for its timber business and sawmills. Despite this, we had a middle-class mentality. This is a mindset I still embody and value, which drives me to put in the hard work for things I want to achieve and be grateful for the things in my life.

My parents, especially my mother, deeply valued education. This association of education with evolution ensured that academic pursuits were prioritised for both my siblings and me. I completed my education at a Hindi medium school and lacked the exposure one would get in a big city school at that time.

I initially got into an engineering college in a small town called Gondia, but I left soon after due to a nagging feeling of homesickness. I had always been close to my family, and their absence was a source of anxiety for me. Eventually, I enrolled in a B.Sc. programme at Dr Hari Singh Gour University in Sagar, which was close to my hometown, and completed my three-year degree.

As a local pursuing higher education, I gained a certain prominence in the town. During this period, I was somewhat active in local politics. However, my perspective shifted in my final year when I started to think seriously about my future. My mother, whose blessings are always with me, put her foot down and prevented me from joining our family business. She wanted me to study further and build a life for myself on my own terms. At that time, pursuing an MBA was highly regarded, so I started preparing for the entrance exams. In the interim, I enrolled in a one-year diploma course in Indore focused on export–import management. As I finished the course, I cleared the Management Aptitude Test (MAT) and eventually earned my MBA degree.

During my MBA, I landed an internship with ABCL but, unfortunately, the company couldn't commit to a full-time position after my internship ended. Subsequently, I got an opportunity in Dubai, working as a marketing executive for a company called Alpha, specialising in business media. However, due to visa complications, I had to return to India.

After a couple of months in Chhindwara, I relocated to Delhi in search of employment. A relative referred me to Mr Samir Kale, founder of CMCG, a renowned PR firm at the time. I gained valuable experience over the next few years with Samir. Monetarily, it was a considerable step down—in Dubai,

I earned a monthly salary of 7000 Dirhams (plus incentives) as opposed to ₹7,200 in Delhi.

During my first interview with Samir, he asked what I knew about PR. I replied that it was about media management, sharing my experience from ABCL, where I managed the registration desk for press conferences. Impressed by my detailed response, he hired me, marking the beginning of my career in PR, which I often describe as happening by chance rather than by choice.

My incredibly rich tenure at CMCG, spanning the next three years, saw me handling top broadcast clients including ESPN Star Sports, Cartoon Network, HBO, CNN, TNT, Turner Group and Channel V.

Subsequent to this engagement, I worked at Genesis with Prema and Ashwani. Prema's role in my professional life is of a teacher who instilled in me humility and passion for my work. At Genesis, under Prema's mentorship, I learnt the essence of relationship-building, fundamental to our field of PR. Ashwani's strategic acumen, on the other hand, taught me structured thinking and crafting meticulous strategies.

With initiatives like the Genesis Foundation, I learnt the importance of social responsibility. At Kaizzen, our involvement in impactful social initiatives has served as invaluable life lessons for all of us.

I carried these skills and values to my final exclusive engagement with an outside body, The Energy and Resources Institute (TERI). There I started out as an advisor of communications, eventually leading the communications team as the director. After a rich tenure at TERI, I moved on to establish Kaizzen.

The two main drivers for starting Kaizzen were my friend circle and the encouragement from my professional network.

Friends constantly nudged me to start my own business, believing in my potential. Meanwhile, former bosses from Genesis, CMCG and other connections in the profession often sought my advice and assistance, highlighting a demand for my expertise.

Interestingly, I wasn't the first employee of Kaizzen. After moving on from TERI, I registered the company and hired Neha Saxena, who worked from the client's office. We secured two clients even before the company's name was officially registered. We organised an event before the company was fully set up. During the initial phases, while I was still with TERI, I helped build the team. We registered Kaizzen on 11 April 2008, and by July, we were operational. I joined full-time in August, with three clients: Learn Asia, a real estate company called Aren and the Embassy of Sweden.

Initially, we faced significant financial challenges. At one point, my wife and I had only ₹142 in our account. It seemed like a setback then, exacerbated by bad debts totalling up to ₹25 lakhs in the second year alone.

However, something interesting happened. When I started Kaizzen, I received many calls from friends, both within and outside the fraternity. A few showed scepticism, saying, 'Let's wait and watch, it's a matter of time.' While I was on the verge of closing up shop, I couldn't shake off the feeling that this was not the end. I did not want to give those sceptics the satisfaction of seeing me fail. I decided to close the Bangalore office and focus on rebuilding the Delhi office. With just two employees and two clients, we slowly started rebuilding Kaizzen.

Since then, we have grown significantly, nearly eightfold in the last four years. We now have a dedicated team focused on educational work, producing white papers and conducting research known as Kaizzen Insights. Our social media team is growing steadily, with increasing activity in that area and our compounding influencer engagement. We have built a comprehensive 360-degree team, allowing us to sign clients in one vertical and then cross-sell our services. This strategy has been highly effective for Kaizzen so far.

Let me remind you what the term *kaizzen* means—'continuous improvement'. This mindset was an enabler for the Japanese, who rebuilt an entire economy out of the ashes post World War II. We, at Kaizzen, attach significant value to facilitating good change that fits in the big picture.

The core of Kaizzen is our value system—our principles are the North Star of our journey. One such compass is ethics, which forms our interactions with people (both internal and external) and our business operations. For instance, when it comes to resource optimisation, the overall long-term value proposition would outweigh the quick fix of cutting corners.

All pragmatism requires a cohesion mechanism, a glue of sorts, for an organisation to become humane. Our binding material is kindness. If we view the world with the lens of interconnectedness, each action snowballs into consequences. Therefore, compassion and kindness are central to Kaizzen's being. Our social activities are a way to share with and serve those who are struggling to fend for themselves. This helps us stay grounded and become centred. We make sure our teams stay connected to the ground reality and understand their role in the overall scheme of things. This centring encourages creativity and innovation.

We value our people, truly. For us, growth is not an isolated journey but a grand carnival of all our people inching towards our best, together. We maintain a very healthy retention ratio for our employees, which is a matter of pride for us. The iridescent feather in our hat, however, is the retention of our clients. Imagine this: sixteen years later, our first three clients are still with us. We have grown nearly eightfold in the last four years. But our story has just begun.

I work with IDCA and Rise Against Hunger India in numerous ways. These engagements are very close to my heart. While other things are important, my involvement in these organisations nurtures my love for my work.

From Twenty-four Hours to Twenty-four Seconds

In simple terms, the lead time to respond has drastically reduced, shrinking from twenty-four hours to just twenty-four seconds. Two decades ago, we typically had twenty-four hours to build our narrative, smoothen the creases and prepare the spokesperson, especially in times of crisis. Today, however, crises can break on social media, leading to immediate, sometimes instantaneous challenges in managing our narrative.

The chances of success for a business are tied to the geopolitical landscape it navigates in. India presents a unique proposition as a pluralistic, multi-cultural, multi-lingual and diverse society and stands out as one of the few markets in which traditional and new-age media seamlessly coexist. While we have evolved and adapted to changing times, our original values remain deeply rooted, serving as foundations for growth.

In addition to the response lead time, sensitivity is crucial. We live in a hyper-aware world, intricately connected with technology. In the past, many crises went unnoticed, but today's technological advancements demand a swift and appropriate response for every issue. With advanced listening tools, dissemination of information at lightning speed and proliferation of misleading content via social media, there is a reduced margin for complacency. Effective crisis management hinges not only on addressing the issue at hand, but also on resonating with diverse thought-pools by crafting strategic responses that mitigate any present or potential backlash. Such a nuanced approach can only be cultivated through the understanding of cultural sensitivities and the ethical framework, geopolitical scenario and evolving dynamics of public opinion. This agility and get-set-go attitude has become the backbone of PR businesses.

The Future Lies in Data and Authenticity

The most efficient and systematic way to build a lasting reputation is through PR intervention. This was the case earlier, it is the case now and will remain so. There are various ways in which reputation is built. Some of them are as mentioned below:

1. *Seeding authenticity*: Staying true to the core and upholding commitments.
2. *Earned PR and fake news*: In an era of fake news and disinformation, the value of earned PR has increased multi-fold and will continue to be. An integral part of it is also weeding out the deterrents (fake news) to correct information.
3. *AI tools as enablers*: Can AI replace the human touch of how stories are put together? Definitely not! But can we use AI to enhance storytelling, save time on research and deliver interesting viewpoints? Definitely!
4. *Understanding data analysis*: The importance of data and measurable impact is unquestionable. If we do not use

data to read the pulse and adapt our strategies regularly, we might be in for a rude shock.

5. *Harvesting influencer management*: Influencers are a crucial PR tool and there is no stopping the impact and insight that they bring to the table. Whether it's travel or technology, daily use products or luxury goods, influencers bring their own perspective to a product or service and can make or break its reputation. Their influence is predicted to grow further in the coming years. PR firms not only work with established influencers but are also engaged in nurturing those whose impact will ripen in the coming years.
6. *Packaging purpose-led communication*: 'Diversity and Inclusion' (DEI), 'culture', 'sustainability' and 'environment' are not merely buzzwords anymore. Organisations prioritising these areas gain an unmistakable competitive advantage and have a wider resonance with stakeholders.

12

Archana Jain

Founder and CEO of PR Pundit Havas Red

'My journey from a military upbringing to a career in PR has been enriched by the skills I learnt along the way—discipline, adaptability and inclusivity.'

From Market Research to Public Relations

I'M VERY PROUD OF MY FORMATIVE YEARS, WHICH HAVE shaped who I am today. My father served in the Indian Air Force, which meant I grew up in multiple geographies and engaged with various cultures. My military background instilled an innate discipline in me, and my family's frequent relocation taught me the important life skill of adaptability. We had strict rules at home, such as dressing properly for dinner (no PJs) and eating together as a family, which fostered a sense of unity and shared experiences.

Growing up in a military family, we never stayed in one place for more than three or four years. Just as I would establish friendships, it would be time to move to a new school, a new city, and start all over again. This repeated change taught me agility and flexibility, invaluable traits in business. It also exposed me to diverse backgrounds and religions, fostering in me a natural instinct for inclusivity.

These experiences of discipline, adaptability and inclusivity have been pivotal lessons from my upbringing. I attended five different schools, moving from Delhi to Barrackpore, Baroda, Shillong and back to Delhi. Later, I studied at Jesus and Mary College and did my master's in business economics from South Campus—both at Delhi University. After getting married and briefly living overseas, I returned to look for a job in market research but was fortunate to be offered an opportunity to learn and work in PR.

My first job in PR was at Hyatt Regency, Delhi. While I interviewed for an opening in market research, I was offered a PR role. With the support of my employer, I quickly learnt on the job. This role involved managing a three-member graphics team, coordinating with the advertising agency, writing copy and liaising with the media, which was the best training I could have asked for!

After two years in the hotel industry, I felt ready for new challenges and joined Genesis PR in 1992 as their third employee. The hands-on experience at Hyatt Regency was invaluable as I worked closely with the founder, Prema Sagar, to build the practice. The early 1990s were a transformative period in India, a changing economic landscape, an evolution of the private sector as well as the advent of the PR consultancy business. The insurance sector was being liberalised and the automobile sector was modernising, finally offering consumers a choice beyond a Fiat or an Ambassador. This era saw the entry of Daewoo, Hyundai, Samsung and LG into Indian markets. It was also a time when India was exploring the privatisation of electricity and water. Many global companies were eager to establish a presence in India, marking a significant shift in the market. This period was filled with opportunities for brand launches and thought leadership, as well as crisis communication, which kept me energised each day.

Eventually, I moved on to set up my own PR firm, PR Pundit, in 1998.

The B2C aspect of PR particularly fascinated me. At that time, there were few lifestyle publications. Business dailies often covered product launches without delving into the nuances of the products. Drawing on all the lessons and experiences from my earlier roles, I set out to take charge of communications by highlighting the emotional and functional attributes of brands and products.

I recall working with early adopters, who wrote about design, and others who covered fine dining and art. We collaborated with hotels and wine brands like Moët Hennessy to introduce new dining experiences, showcasing the integration of wines into meals. Publications like *The Economic Times* and *Business Standard* provided space to discuss these innovations on their weekend pages.

Our goal was to move beyond mere product listings and emphasise the deeper attributes of brands. This approach helped establish PR Pundit as a pioneer in lifestyle and consumer PR. We gradually built a reputation for creating meaningful content for businesses. A few intuitive figures like Dr Gita Piramal recognised our efforts and connected us with clients like Asian Paints and VIP Bags, allowing us to expand our reach and impact.

In summary, the early years of PR Pundit were marked by our commitment to showcase the value of brands and products in the course of everyday life, fostering a deeper affinity for them. This approach set us apart and helped shape the future of lifestyle and consumer PR in India.

Prospects would question if I was deeply committed to persevering and growing the business. Remember that these were the pre-start-up years, and there were concerns in those days when young people set up new ventures.

My first client was Royal Sun Alliance. The then CEO Antony Jacob trusted me with their PR duties. I used to consult the insurance sector during my tenure at Genesis PR, as numerous insurance companies from all over the world, including Prudential and ING, were exploring opportunities in the Indian market during those years.

However, I had to reflect on what I could do differently to make a mark. Initially, we began to take on projects for notable brands like Moët Hennessy and Swarovski in the early 2000s. As global lifestyle brands started arriving at our shores around 2007–08, the economic outlook for PR Pundit started to change. By then, we had also built a substantial portfolio and developed the talent that they expected in a market like ours. This led to our business gaining momentum.

Strengthening PR Pundit's reputation beyond luxury and lifestyle, we emerged as India's first and only PR company to have won a Gold PR Lion at Cannes in 2017 for our campaign for ITC Savlon.

On Children's Day in 2016, Savlon introduced a set of unique chalk sticks infused with soap suds to engage children at primary schools, to emphasise the importance of washing hands before eating. This innovation was based on an insight—to induce behavioural change among children, the process of communication and education has to be fun, engaging and memorable. Some of the country's biggest news channels featured and lauded the initiative. The PR value earned through exposure across the country was significant and spurred demand for the food grade chalk sticks from schools and NGOs. While the innovation came from the brand, our task was to communicate it effectively far and wide. So it was extremely gratifying when Akshaya Patra, the world's largest provider of mid-day meals in schools, feeding more than a million children every day, knocked on the doors of the brand to ask for Savlon Chalk Sticks. There are many factors that go into how the juries at Cannes select a PR Lion winner, but they certainly evaluate closely, 'Is the work earned, does it live in the culture and did it have an impact?'

Another favourite project is the one undertaken for Jo Malone London and the introduction of the India-inspired Cologne Intense—Jasmine Sambac & Marigold—in April 2018. It offered us a powerful storytelling opportunity and an opportunity to deliver an unconventional fragrance launch! A scented adventure was designed to take key editors, opinion leaders and content creators to the heart of the scent's inspiration—a colourful, chaotic Indian flower market! They were only later introduced to the addictive new Cologne Intense over an indulgent breakfast and an immersive floral box-making activity at the store! We cultivated desire by going beyond editorial coverage by driving emotional and visual storytelling across social media. The creatives were designed around the launch to deliver a unique experience of exclusivity and refinement.

In June 2024, we earned our second PR Lions at Cannes. The Coke Studio Bharat campaign 'Sing to Remember' used the power of music to give under-represented languages a stage to build popular appeal and make them part of pop culture. Strategic and customised PR outreach was deployed for each of the ten songs in different languages. For 'Khalasi' (a traditional Gujarati folk song in a language spoken by less than 5 per cent of India's population), we used the power of influencers, choreographers, creators and singers across India to sing along with hook step renditions, in addition to a media blitzkrieg across national, regional and international titles. During Navaratri, the biggest nine-day Gujarati dance festival, we got a billion people to dance, sing and celebrate the number. We also orchestrated its replay during the closing ceremony of the ICC World Cup 2023 Final at Ahmedabad. The 'Sing to Remember' campaign featuring 'Khalasi' didn't just break the internet, it made history in pop culture, surpassing English and Hindi hits on all the charts. It was the #1 most Shazamed song in India; #3 Spotify daily viral song in India for ninety days; #10 Spotify daily top songs in India for three weeks; globally #8 on Spotify viral charts for two weeks. 'Khalasi' garnered more than five billion views and more than a billion streams. The song and artist earned appreciation from Prime Minister Narendra Modi. The traditional Gujarati folk song continues to feature on the playlist of a diverse audience across India, completing its journey from India to Cannes!

Media Communications Led to an Integrated Approach

Over the thirty-four years that I have spent in the profession, and the twenty-six years since founding PR Pundit, I have witnessed a remarkable evolution and advancement in PR from pure-play press communications to the integrated format being practised today. Initially, we focused merely on media communications. Today, the practice of PR takes a more integrated approach that encompasses paid, owned, shared and earned media. This holistic method enables us to advise clients on leveraging the best combination of these media, making our work infinitely more fulfilling.

The evolution of PR is closely linked to the developments in the media landscape. In the 1990s, business journalism came into its own, providing a springboard for the PR profession and marking the birth of modern-day PR. The turn of the century brought television into the mix, adding a new dimension to our roles. As international lifestyle and luxury brands entered India in 2007–08, the PR landscape witnessed the rise of features and lifestyle media, including global titles, requiring us to adapt our PR strategies to engage broader audiences. The advent of digital media in 2010 marked a significant shift to include blogs and online news outlets as crucial channels for PR programmes. Thereafter in 2015, social media influencers started to become an indispensable part of PR campaigns. The rise of content creators, particularly in consumer tech, travel, fashion and beauty, opened new avenues for brand engagement and storytelling. It was during the accelerated digital migration of 2020 that podcasts started to gain popularity. This shift highlighted the importance of adapting to new formats and staying current with technological trends.

Over the past two decades, the PR profession has grown exponentially. There is a greater understanding and respect for our practice. PR is recognised as a strategic function essential for building and nurturing reputation. Organisations now appreciate PR's role in fostering goodwill and changing consumer behaviour through consistent and relevant communication and believe PR is a necessary function to tell compelling stories and highlight brand values. This has led to a deeper commitment and widespread adoption of integrating PR into the overall business strategies across businesses of all sizes.

A significant and welcome change has been the rise of young professionals in the business. Early in my career, lack of experience was often seen as a drawback. Today, companies value the fresh perspectives and innovative ideas brought by young PR practitioners. This opens doors to promising opportunities for the youth, making our field more dynamic and forward-thinking.

The growth of training institutions, conferences, awards and journals dedicated to PR highlight the development of the profession. These resources provide ongoing education, recognise excellence and foster a sense of community among PR professionals.

Adapting to Consumer Expectations, Media Disruptions and Technological Opportunities

Drawing inspiration from Taylor Swift, the PR profession is poised to 'keep cruisin'' despite challenges. While detractors may continue to criticise the profession, PR professionals will 'shake it off' and continue to innovate and excel. Having the pulse of the 'now and the new' is critical in our profession. The future of PR lies in our ability to keep pace with rapidly evolving consumer expectations, disruptions in the media landscape and opportunities offered by technology to sharpen our communication programme. Failure to do so is to risk obsolescence.

The concept of integrated communications is promising, providing a level playing field for PR consultants to score across PR, digital, media, influencer, social and creative. This requires us to pivot in our thinking beyond mere PR to advise brands on positioning, marketing, experientials, etc. A change in the traditional mindset of practitioners is imperative to model behaviour and advisory as expected from organisations. It is time therefore to redefine our value proposition and cascade it across the fraternity and in the education system. As we navigate this ever-changing landscape, our ability to differentiate wisely and cultivate a strong presence and image for our profession will be crucial for our success.

Authentic storytelling will remain at the heart of our PR profession and will determine our future too. But we will need to be increasingly more culturally sensitive as we curate credible stories to impact change and communities. Big brands have had to ward off angry trolls and withdraw campaigns such as MakeMyTrip's open offer to our neighbour's cricket fans.

While creativity may be the currency of an integrated model in this digital and social world, building genuine relationships with audiences and communities is crucial. People find authentic content and recommendations by actual consumers more trustworthy than promotions and advertising by brands. We must therefore not leave community advocacy to chance, but step in to help craft and manage a meaningful brand advocacy strategy. This set of loyal and vocal customers helps humanise brands, boost brand appeal and trust, promote products and services, provide invaluable user-generated social media chatter and word-of-mouth recommendations.

Understanding and integrating environmental, social and corporate governance (ESG) principles into PR strategies is essential too. The reputation of an organisation increasingly depends on how it engages with its employees, demonstrates dedication to sustainability and addresses broader social issues. PR practitioners must therefore be well-versed in ESG to offer relevant solutions and highlight a company's commitment to these values.

The future of PR also hinges on nurturing a diverse and culturally sensitive workforce. Building inclusive workplaces free from hierarchy, prejudices and bureaucracy is critical to attracting and retaining talent. As a new generation seeks to join purpose-driven organisations, the PR business must consciously foster environments that embrace diversity and cultural sensitivity.

To ensure continued success, PR efforts must be measurable. Demonstrating the value of PR through clear metrics is essential for sustaining growth. Clients must see value in our services and must feel valued by our counsel to become advocates for us, akin to Lady Gaga's dedicated fan base of 'Little Monsters'.

13

Ashish Jalan

Managing Director of Concept PR

'My strategy is straightforward—retain my leadership team and ensure they retain their second-in-command, who, in turn, retain their teams. If everyone stays, I've done something right.'

From Movie Production to Public Relations

I was born in Ranchi, but my family moved to Bombay when I was barely six months old. I studied at Bombay Scottish School and then completed my B.Com from HR College. After that, I pursued chartered accountancy and qualified as a CA. My family was in the garment fabric business, so I worked with my father for a while, but I didn't enjoy it.

Throughout my career, I have explored various fields. For a couple of years, I ran an automobile ancillary unit in Pune. I also did stockbroking and garment exports for a few years. However, I found my true calling when I met Vivek Suchanti. Vivek, a true visionary I greatly admire, has been like a rock in my life. Vivek and I made a movie together prior to launching Concept PR, but it was a major flop. I had decided to go back to my family business when Vivek asked me to try my hand at PR. And the rest is history.

Concept Communications was primarily an ad agency, and PR was limited to IPO-related activities. There wasn't a real PR business to speak of. Given my CA background, I initially wanted to start an investor relations (IR) business. While we did begin with IR, we soon realised that PR fits well with our overall vision.

Concept Communications had existed since 1989 and already had an office. But we initially operated from a small basement office in a nearby building. Soon after, we moved to a larger space in the main office. Concept PR was officially launched in 2005, marking the beginning of our focus on signing clients for their PR mandates. My first client was Gokaldas Exports.

For a while, our company was focused primarily on numbers, emphasising the bottom line over the top line. We had a lean team and weren't investing in the right talent. It was a small group handling everything. About seven to eight years ago, we realised that our main strength was our people. PR isn't like a manufacturing unit, where one person's thoughts can drive the entire operation. It relies on a team of talented individuals.

We understood the importance of hiring the right talent. Vivek often reminded me that we needed to view this as an investment, not a cost. This shift in perspective over the last seven to eight years has made a significant difference, enabling us to attract and retain the right talent, which has been crucial to our success.

Recently, we have successfully recruited exceptional talent, leading to significant growth in our management and leadership team. What was once a core group of four or five individuals over many years has now expanded to over twenty capable team members. We are continuously searching for individuals who fit our vision, and I take a hands-on approach in the interview process. Finding and welcoming the right people aboard brings me immense satisfaction.

We place a lot of importance on retention, both for clients and employees. While acquiring new clients is crucial, nurturing and consolidating relationships with existing clients is equally vital. We pride ourselves on maintaining long-standing partnerships, some spanning over a decade. On the employee front, being recognised as a 'Great Place to Work' speaks volumes of our commitment to them.

Another path to growth has been recognising the need to evolve. The digital team, which was just a handful before the pandemic, has now become a crucial part of our operations. These twenty-five to thirty-year-olds are incredibly smart and confident, and I love how they are not afraid to knock on my door and have a chat. Despite our growing size, we maintain a flat organisational structure where everyone knows I'm accessible. There's a formal process in place, but no hierarchy in terms of spirit. Interestingly, the younger team members readily come in to talk, while some of the older ones might be a bit more hesitant. For instance, we recently had an intern who joined us. She came in to thank me for the opportunity, introducing herself confidently and expressing her happiness with the experience. She even mentioned wanting to return next year for another stint, which was really gratifying.

This openness and accessibility have become integral to our culture. We recognise the importance of bringing young talent on board and giving them responsibility and authority. Allowing them to take the lead on projects has proven to be very effective.

My strategy is straightforward—retain my leadership team and ensure they retain their second-in-command, who, in turn, retain their teams. If everyone stays, I have done something right. Whether it means taking the team out for a drink, a movie, inviting them over or just being there in times of need, I'm committed to fostering a strong bond between us.

I believe that even if someone gets a higher raise elsewhere, they won't leave us because it's not just about the money—it's about how they are treated. This approach isn't purely for work; it's about building a genuine connection. I enjoy coming to the office and don't dread Monday mornings. Without this bond, it would all just feel like work. Instead, it's easy to come to the office, sit down with anyone for a cup of coffee and chat about goals, making the workday enjoyable.

I would also like to point out that I have been a sportsman all my life, enjoying football, cricket, badminton and chess. You name the sport, and I have probably played it. It's something I really enjoy. I still stay active and play sports, though not as intensely as I used to. For instance, if I play football now, it takes me a couple of days to recover. But I keep up with my activities and exercise regularly. Staying active and fit is something I have always prioritised, and it keeps me going.

I always advise my colleagues to maintain a balanced life. I often tell them to strive for this balance because, in my own experience, I was so busy working hard that I sometimes feel like I didn't give enough time to my family.

Of the many memorable campaigns we have managed over the years, one campaign that remains etched in my memory is

'Save Campa Cola Compound', a remarkable undertaking that showcases the holistic use of media for advocacy. The Campa Cola Compound residents were abruptly served notices of demolition by the BMC in 2012, impacting 200 families.

We embarked on a multifaceted campaign, weaving traditional PR channels—television, print and radio—with the dynamic landscape of digital media, pioneering what is now recognised as integrated communication. The rallying cry echoed across platforms, from X (formerly Twitter), where the hashtag #SaveCampaCola gained traction, to online petitions on Change.org, galvanising support from far and wide.

Yet, it was not just virtual solidarity that defined our campaign. On ground, we arranged a symphony of activism, orchestrating a protest march to the chief minister's bungalow and human chains bearing messages of the injustice. From the emotional debate on the *Arnab Goswami Show* to the spotlight of global news networks, including the USA and the Middle East, the plight of Worli's residents became a symbol of resilience and collective action.

Our advocacy was acknowledged, with accolades in the national and international arenas, affirming the power of holistic and integrated movements to effect change.

All Aboard the Rollercoaster Called PR

Get ready for a nostalgic trip down memory lane! Imagine yourself in the late 1990s, a time when PR professionals ruled the media kingdom armed with nothing but press releases and an endless supply of fax paper.

Ah, those were the days! They paraded around like royalty, mastering the art of conveying their message through traditional channels.

Fast forward to the early 2000s, when the PR scene was as predictable as a saas–bahu soap opera. Press conferences were the talk of the town, and landing a feature in *The Economic Times* was the Holy Grail of publicity. Those were simpler times, when the only social media available was a catch-up with the neighbourhood aunty over a cup of chai and a few samosas.

But then, like a plot twist in a Bollywood flick, the digital revolution happened. Suddenly, PR pros found themselves in uncharted territory, grappling with the complexities of hashtags, retweets and viral videos. It was like trying to teach your grandmother to use WhatsApp—confusing, chaotic and occasionally hilarious.

Zoom into the 2020s, where screens reign supreme, and the internet is our playground. Social media emerged as a game changer for modern PR, offering brands unprecedented opportunities to connect with audiences in ways previously unimaginable. No more sending messages via carrier pigeons—now it's all about crafting viral tweets, collaborating with Instagram influencers and unboxing products on YouTube. Old-timers struggle to adapt to this newly transformed digital world of technological evolution, use tools to increase efficiency, use data-crunched strategy for effectiveness and use post-implementation analytics to measure ROI. Ah, the good old days!

And then, just when they thought they had seen it all, the mother of all plot twists came: the COVID-19 pandemic. Suddenly, PR pros were thrust into the spotlight like never before, juggling crisis communication, remote work and endless Zoom meetings. With this arose the debate on the efficiency of 'WFH' or the work-from-home culture.

But amidst the chaos of hashtags and viral trends, one thing remained constant: the power of a good story. Whether it's a tale of triumph or a saga of redemption, PR pros discovered that authenticity was the key to winning over even the most sceptical audiences, transforming them into loyal followers. Content is still king!

Finally, as we embark on our journey into the future, let's raise our unicorn mugs to the PR pros who dared to dream big and spin tales worthy of winning likes and followers. Who knows what adventures lie ahead? So, grab your smartphones and hold onto your hashtags—this digital rollercoaster is just getting started!

Embracing the Integrated Future

The world has witnessed a profound transformation in the first two decades of the twenty-first century, and the coming years will be no different. Our profession and its practitioners will also have to anticipate and adapt to the many changes. However, the one overarching trend that I foresee is the need for integrated communication. Operating in isolated silos will inevitably lead to redundancy. So, here's my advice to the communication professionals.

Forging tomorrow's PR landscape together: In a world where every day seems to bring a new technological marvel and shifts in how people connect, PR is going through a real transformation. While we still hold onto the tried-and-tested methods of the past, we are also looking towards a future where PR is a beautiful blend of different ways to communicate. Integrated communication isn't just a buzzword; it's the melody that weaves together PR, both organic and inorganic, advertising, digital media and more into a symphony of connection.

The journey towards integration: We are moving away from the days of doing PR in a bubble. Instead, we are realising the magic of intertwining PR seamlessly with marketing and advertising. While we definitely still value old-school PR essentials, the path ahead is all about embracing a more intricate strategy. Integrated communication embraces a whole range of tactics, from crafting engaging content and building relationships on social media to teaming up with influencers and diving deep into data analytics. It eliminates the distinctions between paid media, earned media, advertising and PR; instead, it prioritises communication to achieve the objective of the campaign. With this holistic approach, PR pros can create campaigns that really hit home with audiences while also expanding reach and impact.

Technology, the catalyst: Technology isn't just changing the game—it's setting the stage for a whole new kind of performance. With fancy tools for analytics, AI-driven insights and platforms that automate processes, PR pros now have access to efficiencies unimaginable earlier. They can dig deep into data, personalise the messages and make sure that the campaigns are firing on all cylinders. By embracing these technological marvels, organisations open up new avenues for engagement and stay nimble in a digital world that's always on the move.

Cultivating collaboration and cross-functional teams: However, all this tech wizardry isn't worth much if they do not work together as a team. It's important to build teams with professionals from PR, advertising and the digital domain. Collaboration isn't just about getting the job done; it's about sparking innovation and staying ahead of the curve in a world that never stops changing.

As the world of PR evolves, those of us who embrace integrated communication are going to come out on top. By breaking free from the confines of traditional PR and embracing a multifaceted approach, we can navigate the twists and turns of the digital age with grace and resilience. Integrated communication isn't just a strategy, it's a journey—one that celebrates teamwork, harnesses the power of technology and leads us towards meaningful connections in an ever-changing world.

14

Zacharia James

Founding Partner of Six Degrees, Currently Investor and Partner, The PRactice

'I always say I've been blessed with three things: the ability to keep my feet on the ground, knowing my strengths and weaknesses and the gift of attracting talented people.'

Moving from Panjim to New Delhi

I am originally from Kerala, but I was brought up in Goa. I did my schooling at Don Bosco in Panjim.

I was not very academically inclined as a child—my focus was always more on sports, and I spent a lot of my time playing basketball. One of the most impactful experiences was the community service culture that Don Bosco instilled in us. We eventually moved to Delhi in 1987, which was an interesting change for me. The culture in Delhi was very different from what I was used to in Goa. I made new friends, and it changed my personality. In Delhi, I started to pay more attention to academics and general knowledge. I became more aware.

My father was a bureaucrat, and we lived on Kasturba Gandhi Marg. It was an apartment complex that housed families with backgrounds in defence and civil services. This exposure had a significant influence on me. My real coming of age was somewhere around 1990, and I started to get more serious about my career, though I was still unsure about what I wanted to pursue.

After completing my graduation in political science, I pursued a post-graduation in PR from Bharatiya Vidya Bhavan. During that time, my brother, who was in advertising, pointed me to an ad in the newspaper for a job at Perfect Relations. It was for a written test and group interview in Noida. I got through the written test and group interview. On 1 October 1994, I had an interview and was offered a job with a salary of ₹3,500 per month. They had me start immediately, even though the next day was Gandhi Jayanti. That pretty much set the tone of my work culture and focus for several years.

My introduction to PR and Perfect Relations was pivotal. The foundation I built there was incredibly strong, teaching me resilience and persistence. I'm grateful to Dilip and Bobby, with whom I worked closely. I soon started working with senior people like Tarun Deo and Sudip Mozumder, and it was a great experience.

Early in my career, I was involved in some fascinating campaigns for clients like BBC, CNN and American Express. These campaigns were particularly significant because it was early days for the foreign electronic media in the Indian market. Working with Motorola was also interesting, as they were introducing paging devices for communication and soon after, mobile and cellular phones.

I was fortunate to work on such a diverse mix of clients and exciting projects. One highlight was our collaboration with

Turner International. We worked on a campaign for Cartoon Network, marking the first visit of Mickey Mouse to India at Appu Ghar in New Delhi. It was a major campaign with front-page reportage across various publications.

In my career, I have been involved in several interesting campaigns. For instance, I worked with Eduardo Faleiro, who was an MP and a minister in the Congress government from Goa. These experiences have been instrumental in shaping my professional journey.

Tarun Deo got me into Text100 (now known as Archetype), where I worked for several years. I joined as an account director and eventually became the managing director and president for the Text100 Group in India. I have always preferred staying in India and have never been excited about moving abroad. This preference somewhat limited my growth opportunities with global organisations, as advancement beyond a certain level typically required relocation outside India. This was when I decided to move on despite the support of Aedhmar Hynes, the then CEO of Text100, and Tim Dyson, the then CEO of Next Fifteen, the parent company.

So, I quit and set up my own firm. My goal was to apply the successful models I had developed at Text100 to my new venture. I was fortunate to meet Barry French, the global head of communications for Nokia Networks, where I worked as a consultant to their global head office in Finland for six months. In 2008, I set up Alphabet Consulting, a firm specialising in content solutions and internal communications, and we secured a long-term contract with Nokia Networks.

In 2009, Rishi Seth and I launched Six Degrees, following which Rishi joined Alphabet as a partner too. Our initial clients at Six Degrees were the Hughes and Bird Group, thanks to our strong past relationships with Pranav Roach and the Bhatia family respectively.

Rishi and I brought the agility and can-do attitude from our Perfect Relations days and combined it with the strong systems and methodologies that we learnt at Text100. We managed to find the sweet spot between these two work cultures, which helped us realise significant success in client retention and satisfaction at both Alphabet and Six Degrees.

Initially, most of our clients were in the technology sector, but within a couple of years, we expanded to non-tech sectors, which became a significant growth area for us. This diversification was a major win, as we were initially known predominantly in the tech space.

We were fortunate to attract talented people who had worked with us before across both the firms. Key hires such as Garima Misra, Karan Punia, Deepika Bansal, Kiran Balasubramanium joined us, contributing significantly to our success. I always say I have been blessed with three things: the ability to keep my feet on the ground, knowing my strengths and weaknesses and the gift of attracting talented people. Our people have been responsible for helping build the reputation we have enjoyed over the years, while we ensured our gratitude was conveyed to them, leading to a win-win situation for everyone involved.

In addition, our success is also largely credited to the great clients we worked with, such as Paroma Roy Chowdhury, Meenu Handa and Gaurav Bhaskar at Google, Shiv Shivakumar and Poonam Kaul at Nokia, Rajiv Kaul at CMS InfoSystems and Nivedeeta Moirangthem at IKEA, amongst others.

I like to pace my growth, and this approach is reflected in the way Alphabet and Six Degrees have evolved. There were many business opportunities we could have pursued, but we often chose not to if we felt they would disrupt the work culture within our organisation. Even though some of these opportunities could have brought in significant revenue, we felt that they didn't align with our values.

When it comes to hiring, we believe the responsibility lies with us if things don't work out. If someone leaves their job to join us and then isn't able to integrate into our company, it's on us for not assessing the fit properly. We encourage our team to invest time and effort in helping new hires succeed. There have been instances where, despite our best efforts, things didn't work out. In such cases, we aim to be fair and give individuals ample time to find something else.

Our approach to people management is rooted in respect and fairness. We treat everyone with dignity, whether it's our employees, support staff or vendors. Keeping our feet on the ground and respecting everyone is crucial. This attitude fosters a positive and supportive environment, which I believe is the key to our success and growth.

Embracing the Tech Revolution

In recent years, the Indian PR and marketing communications profession has undergone a seismic shift, driven by technological advancements, evolving consumer behaviour and changing media landscapes. This revolution is not just an evolution; it's a complete transformation, redefining how businesses communicate and connect with their audiences. To stay relevant, consultancies must adapt swiftly to these changes, leveraging new tools and strategies to thrive in this dynamic environment.

Digital transformation: Traditional media, once the cornerstone of PR strategies, has been overshadowed by digital platforms. Social media, blogs, podcasts and influencer marketing have become indispensable, allowing businesses to engage directly with audiences. This democratisation of media is a game changer, enabling even small businesses to tell their stories and reach vast audiences without the need for substantial budgets.

For consultancies, therefore, operations and strategies need to fully integrate digital tools and platforms, necessitating investments in digital marketing and social media management.

Data-driven precision: Big data and analytics have revolutionised PR and marketing communications, making them more precise and measurable. Brands can now leverage data to understand consumer behaviour, track campaign performance and make informed decisions.

Consultancies must build robust data analytics capabilities to provide clients with actionable insights. This requires investing in tools and talent capable of analysing vast amounts of data, optimising campaigns in real time and demonstrating clear ROI in an increasingly competitive market.

The blurring lines of IMC: The boundaries between PR, marketing and advertising have blurred, giving rise to integrated marketing communications (IMC). For PR firms, this means offering integrated solutions that combine PR, digital marketing, advertising and content creation.

Collaboration across different teams and disciplines is essential. Consultancies need to foster environments where PR specialists, digital marketers, data analysts and creatives work together seamlessly. This integrated approach not only enhances the effectiveness of campaigns but also provides a unified voice for brands in a fragmented media landscape.

The power of influencers: Influencers with authentic and relatable content enjoy significant followings and can sway consumer opinions and drive engagement.

Consultancies must constantly explore new platforms, adopt creative approaches, stay abreast of the latest trends and understand the nuances of different social media platforms.

Investing in talent and training: The rapid pace of technological advancement requires PR firms to invest in the continuous learning and upskilling of its employees, focusing on digital marketing, data analytics, AI and other emerging technologies.

In addition, in an era where information spreads instantaneously on social media, managing a brand's reputation has become more complex and critical. PR professionals must adopt a proactive approach to crisis management, staying agile and responsive to effectively manage crises and protect brand reputations.

Relevant training and development programmes not only enhance the consultancy's capabilities and ensure PR professionals remain relevant in their roles but also foster innovation and creativity, which should be at the heart of every firm's strategy to stay competitive.

Adapting business models: Consultancies may need to rethink their business models to remain competitive. Traditional retainer-based models will need to be more flexible and align the consultancy's interests with client goals, whereby they demonstrate a commitment to delivering results.

New Era of Engagement and Connectivity

Looking ahead, the fusion of technology and creativity promises to unlock new possibilities. AI and automation will continue to drive change, enhancing efficiency and enabling personalised interactions. AR and VR will provide immersive experiences, transforming consumer engagement. Hyper-personalisation, driven by sophisticated data collection and analysis, will become the norm, fostering deeper connections and enhancing brand loyalty.

The fusion of technology and creativity is not just an opportunity; it is a necessity. Consultancies must embrace this change, adapt their business models and foster innovation to thrive in this dynamic environment.

As we ride the tech waves into the digital horizon, the key to success lies in our ability to evolve, innovate and stay ahead of the curve. The revolution is here, and it is reshaping the very fabric of PR and marketing communications. It's time to embrace the change, and the future belongs to those who lead the way into a new era of engagement and connectivity.

15

Samir Kale

Founder of Communications Management Consulting Group (CMCG), currently promoter, Mango Village Guhagar

'Our focus was always on retaining clients rather than chasing after new ones every day.'

From Struggling Fresher to Two-time Founder

I'm from Thane, where I have lived my entire life and still reside. My mother was a teacher and my father a mechanical engineer. I attended Saraswati Secondary School, a Marathi medium school that is just about 200 m from my home. After that, I went to B.N. Bandodkar College of Science, commonly known as Thane College, where I earned a degree in physics.

After graduating, I spent a couple of years exploring various businesses, including screen printing, to find my path. Eventually, I realised the need for further education to advance my career. I enrolled in a course in advertising and PR at Symbiosis in Pune, driven by my longstanding interest in advertising. This interest was sparked by my elder sister, who graduated from the Sir J.J. School of Art and was involved in commercial art, which fascinated me and drew me to the field of communications and advertising.

After completing my course, I realised it was time to find a good job. I applied to a few ad agencies that were in business at the time, but they told me I didn't have enough experience. I accepted that and moved on. I then joined Wipro to sell computers. About a month later, I got a call from Roger Pereira—he said that I had applied to their firm six months earlier but never followed up. I went to meet him, and the company offered me a job, though the salary was only about one-sixth or one-seventh of what I was making at Wipro. I accepted the offer without hesitation because I was determined to get into the PR profession.

I worked with Roger Pereira Communications for a little over three years before moving on. In 1993, I joined IPAN and was tasked with starting their Mumbai office. I vividly remember joining in April 1993, just after the bomb blasts in the city. I remember driving from Sewri to downtown and seeing the smoke rising from the blasts. I left IPAN in October 1994. I have always had the drive to be independent—I didn't want to work for someone else. That is why I had explored various small businesses earlier in my career. When I left IPAN, I was ready to start my own venture. Around that time, Enron offered me a job, but I told them I couldn't join them because I was starting my own business. They responded by saying, 'Okay, we'll be your client.' And that's how I got into business.

When I had to send Enron my first invoice, they asked for the company name, and I realised I didn't have one yet. I quickly thought, 'What do we do? Let's call it Communication Management Consulting.' But since I was the only person and there was no company at that point, I wanted the name to sound more established. To make it seem like a larger entity, I decided to add 'Group' to the name. That's how Communication Management Consulting Group (CMCG) came to be. And that's how we started.

The association with Enron gave us credibility. When other American companies heard we were working with them, they saw us as the right company to partner with. This led to us signing on clients like General Motors, PepsiCo, Turner and CNN. These became the mainstay of our business.

Our first employee was a friend of mine, Geeta Seth, who had recently moved to Mumbai from Pune. We had stayed in touch since we were both in the same course in Pune, and when we were talking one day, she mentioned she was open to new opportunities. I said, 'If you're interested, I'd love to have you join me.' And that's how she became part of the team.

For twenty years, our offices were around Shivaji Park in Mumbai. We moved locations a few times, but we stayed in that area because it was centrally located for our team, whether they were commuting from the north or the south. At that time, BKC wasn't developed as a business hub, so Shivaji Park was an ideal spot.

We remained there until 2014, when I decided to step away from the business. So, yes, I ran the firm for exactly twenty years—from 1994 to 2014.

We had only had the Mumbai office for about a year when around 1996 or 1997—I can't recall the exact year—ESPN approached us. They had an office in Delhi and wanted us to pitch for their business. I told them we didn't have a Delhi office and wasn't sure if we could adequately service them. They assured me not to worry and invited us to pitch anyway. We went through two or three rounds of pitching, even meeting with their global team. Eventually, they decided they wanted to work with us, and that's how we ended up opening our office in Delhi. Thereafter, we opened offices in Bangalore and Chennai as well.

When I turned fifty, I decided it was time to step away from the business. Everyone was shocked—how could I do that while still running a successful company? Clients were surprised when I told them I no longer wanted to work with them. But that's exactly what I did. I gave them enough time and motivation to find another firm. After twenty years of being on my own, living out of hotels and airplanes, I realised I didn't want to spend the rest of my life that way. Money is important, but it's not everything. So, I exited the business. My family was stunned, and everyone around me asked me, 'What are you doing?' But I knew it was the right decision for me.

However, the urge to do something of my own didn't just disappear. I bought a piece of land with the initial plan of not doing much—just growing mango trees and maybe some farming. But that eventually evolved into a thriving real estate and hospitality business. Now, I'm deeply involved in this new venture, spending a lot of time on the land. I have even stopped reading newspapers! However, I highly recommend reading newspapers to young PR professionals and everyone else in the business.

I'm truly content with what I'm doing now because at CMCG we accomplished everything we set out to achieve. That's all I needed. Our focus was always on retaining clients rather than chasing after new ones every day. We never aimed to pitch to a hundred clients at once; that wasn't our goal. We worked with many of our clients for ten, twelve, even fifteen years, which is rare these days. Despite changes in leadership at the client organisation, with three different CEOs over the years, our relationships remained strong. It's uncommon to find that level of consistency today.

But those were the times we could manage to retain clients for years. And most people associated us with those brands rather than the people within those organisations. We would put a tremendous amount of effort into each assignment, going far beyond just media-related work. We really immersed ourselves in our clients' businesses, and that made a significant difference to our output. We didn't just work on one or two campaigns. Our relationships with companies lasted much longer, which meant we experienced all the ups and downs together.

Our deep involvement in our clients' businesses led to many memorable experiences. For instance, we worked on the broadcast bill issue for Star TV, a client we supported for many years. We focused solely on that issue for five to six years until the government decided to pull back and revise the bill, which would have otherwise severely impacted the business. It was a critical time for the industry.

We also developed a crisis manual for Ford India that was circulated throughout their offices, and many considered it quite unique. These are just a few examples, but there were many instances where we took a different approach from the norm. Understanding the media landscape and how people react to various issues was crucial for us. Often, the most valuable outcomes were the crises we helped avoid, even though those actions weren't visible to the public. The true impact of our work was sometimes what didn't happen—situations where our advice prevented a potential problem.

There are countless incidents where we recommended against a certain action, and because our clients followed that advice, they avoided significant issues. Those moments are interesting and remind me of the unique role we played in our clients' successes.

PR Helps Business Growth

A lot has changed over the last two decades. The focus of media has shifted from traditional to digital and social. The consumption of content has been altered, with people now having extremely small attention spans. The political battlelines have become sharp, noisy and divisive. Most century-old laws and regulations in India are yet to be revised with clarity and a clear implementation plan. With a stunning advancement in technologies, both urban and rural consumption patterns have been dramatically altered. With a lot more international integration and supply chains, global issues are impacting businesses on a day-to-day basis. And India today is on the verge of becoming the third largest economy in the world. Phew!

That's a hell of a lot to absorb and adopt even for trained and experienced PR professionals. But PR has survived, adapted and is in fact thriving thanks to some serious efforts put in by people from the profession. Here's what I have observed having spent a decade each inside and outside the profession.

Awareness and acceptance: PR is much more widely accepted today as an essential tool by much smaller or even retail businesses when compared to a couple of decades ago, when only international or large Indian businesses considered hiring PR professionals or consultancies. This acceptance coinciding with the exponential growth in the Indian economy has led to the growth of PR as a profession, as we see it today.

Embracing the changing media landscape: In the early days, the role of PR was restricted mostly to managing free publicity in print and television media by building relationships with journalists. Medianet by *The Times of India* group changed that, with media owners realising that they can generate a separate revenue stream by selling editorial space. PR professionals had to change accordingly and take on a more media advisory, perception management role within businesses.

With the decline of traditional media and the advent of social and digital media in the last decade, the role of PR has changed drastically. Understanding technology and media consumption patterns has become a prerequisite for a PR professional. One has to anticipate issues, understand implications and respond at lightning speed. The profession overall has adapted well to this change. The deep penetration of digital media into the rural heartlands of the country has extended the demand for PR services geographically and linguistically.

Business contribution: Over the years, I see more and more PR professionals taking elevated roles in the management decision-making process and even across functional areas. They are developing a far greater understanding of social, political, economic and regulatory issues, and how each of them impacts industries and businesses. Businesses too have realised the substantial contributions they are making in setting and achieving business goals. As a result, the PR profession is attracting excellent talent for both in-house and consultancy roles and expanding rapidly.

The Future is Weirdly Unpredictable

The future is weirdly unpredictable, it is said. And today, it does look really weird, with advancements in technologies such as artificial intelligence and machine learning, Web 3, virtual reality and augmented reality, internet of things, robotics, gene editing, bio printing and many more. With several industries and professions predicted to go extinct, how will PR manage to cope with these changes is certainly worth pondering over.

Let's look back for a moment. About thirty years ago, when I started CMCG, there was no internet, no mobile phones and no email! The fact that workplaces existed in that environment seems almost implausible. They did, and we worked as effectively, if not as efficiently, as we do now. The world of course has changed much in the last three decades and is predicted to change exponentially faster in the coming ones.

Let's analyse the impact of one of these technologies on PR. For example, artificial intelligence and machine learning. AI/ML can simply take over key aspects of the day-to-day tasks of a PR professional, such as data sourcing, consumption and analysis, or message personalisation and targeting. The speed and the accuracy of AI/ML in these and many such tasks will be unmatched by human resources.

However, it will be impossible for AI/ML to clone human intelligence, emotions and creativity. PR professionals will need to maximise the use of these powerful AI tools to create insightful campaigns that evoke human emotions and achieve the desired business results. The objectives of the PR campaigns will still be to build trust based on mutual understanding and respect. I doubt AI will ever manage to transcend this human faculty.

The role of PR professionals then will be to continuously monitor and decipher the impact of issues thrown up by data across business activities; develop strategic, targeted and personalised messaging; identify and quickly develop creative campaigns that help evoke emotions and make an impact on the audiences; and help build lasting relationships in the era of extremely short attention spans. PR professionals will also need to invest time and energy in developing an understanding of regulatory issues and business crises in this changed environment and be able to manage them.

In short, the basics of PR will remain the same in the future. The change will come from the way the inputs are received, analysed and presented and the way professionals use these inputs to deliver targeted, personalised messages across geographies and linguistic boundaries. PR professionals will have to embrace and adapt to the fast-changing technological environment to stay on top. As is the case in several other sectors, I'm sure India will not only produce world-class PR professionals but also soon establish a leadership position in providing PR services to global businesses.

16

Bobby Kewalramani

Co-founder of Perfect Relations

'When we started, we were among the pioneers in the business.'

It was a Leap into the Unknown

My father was an IPS officer and chose the Uttar Pradesh cadre when he joined the civil services. I was born in Meerut, where he was the SP, and spent my early years until the age of ten in various districts of UP. Afterwards, he moved to the central government, and we spent a few years in Delhi. I completed my schooling at an Irish Christian Brothers school in Shillong, which is now in Meghalaya but was then part of Assam.

After passing my ISC in 1971, I enrolled into St Stephen's College, Delhi University, in July 1972. I graduated with a BA Honours in Economics in 1975, then pursued my master's at the Delhi School of Economics. I worked with several media houses, including *The Times of India*, *Sunday Mail* and *Sunday Observer*. Through these experiences, I gained a deep understanding of what makes news and newspapers successful, largely due to the credibility they develop over time.

It was a leap into the unknown. I worked in the sales and marketing department of media houses, and people frequently approached us to get their press releases published and organise press conferences. Around the same time, Dilip Cherian, a classmate from the Delhi School of Economics, and I were both working at the *Observer*. Given the early years of liberalisation under the then Prime Minister Narasimha Rao and the entry of multinationals, we recognised a business opportunity and decided to start our own PR firm. We named it Perfect Relations, with the short-form 'PR' signifying 'Public Relations'. When we started, we were among the pioneers in the business, following IPAN and Good Relations. I believe we were the third PR firm to enter the market.

We started from the house of then-member of Parliament, Mr Shibu Soren. Mr Soren had started a newspaper and Dilip was involved with it. We already had an office for the newspaper, so we initially used that space to work from. There were no mobile phones at that time, and getting a phone connection took forever. So we used a PCO at the Press Club to make calls to clients while working out of Mr Soren's house at Rakabganj Road. We launched in September 1992 with PepsiCo as our first client, and the rest, as they say, is history.

Dilip and I shared a strong understanding and complemented each other well. Our employee number one was Archana Sadanand. However, the most difficult challenge we faced while recruiting for Perfect Relations was finding candidates with good writing skills. It seems the younger generation lacks strong writing abilities, which can only be developed through a habit of reading books. My advice is to cultivate this habit because, on a typical day, you might be advising a beverage company in the morning, a telecom company in the afternoon and a retail company in the evening. General knowledge and understanding of various businesses are crucial if you want to succeed in this profession.

PepsiCo had entered the Indian market and was embroiled in a fierce battle. Their executives, despite their expertise, were discussing everything except their core business of chips, beverages and exports. Additionally, the incumbent PR firm was billing them by the hour, and eight months into the contract, the accounts still hadn't been reconciled. We proposed a flat retainer model with no hidden charges, which appealed to the company. After securing the PepsiCo account, we landed other clients such as Alcatel and English Electric. We only grew from strength to strength.

I'm very happy to have been in the right place at the right time. In 1992, multinationals began entering India in a big way thanks to liberalisation, and PR was traditionally driven by these multinationals. We managed to carve out a niche for ourselves amidst this influx.

We initially had very little competition, as both Good Relations and IPAN had international affiliations, unlike our completely homegrown firm. However, we lacked access to the international clients that Good Relations and IPAN enjoyed. Despite this, we managed to hold our own and grew exponentially. From starting with a single office in 1992, we expanded to seventeen offices by 2016, when we sold the company to Dentsu.

Around 1996 or 1997, British American Tobacco (BAT) attempted to replace the Indian management of ITC with their own. ITC had been built by Indians over several decades, and we fought a very memorable battle against this takeover. We succeeded in preserving the Indian management, making it a case study in crisis management. This was during the early stages of our firm, demonstrating how a company with substantial international connections and access to PR firms and advertising agencies was thwarted by the determined efforts of the Indian management and our team.

Between 2003 and 2005, Coca Cola hired us to address significant issues with their plant in Kerala, which was accused of consuming more water than sanctioned, sparking a popular movement against it. Despite our vigorous efforts to combat the opposition, the plant ultimately had to shut down and remained closed until it was repurposed in 2021 for COVID-19. It was a challenging and memorable campaign, involving battles in newspapers, with the panchayats, the Kerala State Government and international press like the BBC.

When we started, there were just three consultancies. Now, the profession has grown exponentially, possibly reaching 300 such firms. Initially, PR was primarily about media relations—drafting press releases, disseminating them via fax, compiling coverage and delivering a dossier to clients for payment. However, PR has evolved significantly. Nowadays, it involves working closely with large corporations to formulate communication strategies, implementing them and operating at the board level. This extends beyond corporations to NGOs, not-for-profit organisations and foundations.

When we started, we often had to explain the difference between PR and advertising in our presentations. Concept selling was a significant part of our job. Now, clients understand the value of PR and have clearer expectations from PR consultancies.

The profession is attracting younger, smarter individuals equipped with the latest tools and technology. Having worked for over forty-five years, I have seen a lot.

From Media Relations to Essential Corporate Strategy

Over the past two decades, the landscape of PR in India has undergone a remarkable transformation. As a pioneer in the business, I have observed this evolution with keen interest, witnessing PR morph from a mere tool of media relations into an indispensable component of corporate strategy.

Twenty years ago, PR in India revolved predominantly around media relations, primarily targeting English-language mainstream media. However, today, PR has transcended its former boundaries to become intricately woven into the fabric of corporate decision-making. In recent years, the integration of PR with marketing has been remarkable, resulting in campaigns that seamlessly blend brand messaging with consumer engagement. Data and analytics serve as the bedrock of this integration, allowing PR professionals to fine-tune their strategies to maximise impact and ROI. One of the most significant shifts in PR practice has been the heightened emphasis on crisis communication.

In today's volatile and interconnected world, where a single misstep can snowball into a full-blown reputation crisis, PR firms work hand-in-hand with top management to navigate the intricate web of public scrutiny. The ability to respond swiftly and effectively to crises has become paramount, underscoring the importance of proactive crisis management strategies. Moreover, the advent of technology has revolutionised the PR landscape, giving rise to a new discipline: social media management. With the explosive growth of internet users in India—from a mere 2 million two decades ago to a staggering 820 million today—platforms like Facebook, LinkedIn and Instagram have emerged as potent tools for communication and brand engagement. While these platforms offer unparalleled reach and immediacy, they also pose challenges such as the decline of traditional media consumption habits like book reading. PR practitioners must adeptly navigate this digital terrain, staying abreast of evolving trends to effectively engage with their target audience.

Another notable trend is the increasing importance of regional language media in PR strategy. With the proliferation of internet access in tier 2 and tier 3 towns, regional language media outlets have gained prominence, presenting both opportunities and challenges for PR professionals. On the one hand, this expansion broadens the potential reach of PR campaigns to previously untapped audiences. On the other hand, it necessitates the localisation of content, requiring PR practitioners to translate materials into relevant local languages to resonate with diverse audiences. This democratisation of media presents a positive trend overall, as it enables brands to connect with a more diverse and inclusive audience base.

Further, the evolution of PR practice has spurred the emergence of media training as a critical component of consultancy offerings. Twenty years ago, media training was virtually non-existent, whereas today it is considered indispensable for effective communication and brand representation. PR firms invest significant resources in honing the media skills of their clients, equipping them with the tools and techniques to navigate interviews, press conferences and other media interactions with confidence and finesse.

The evolution of PR in India over the past two decades has been nothing short of revolutionary. As we look to the future, one thing remains certain: the role of PR will continue to evolve, adapting to the ever-changing dynamics of the media landscape and the needs of its stakeholders. However, the essence of PR remains unchanged: trust. In a world inundated with noise and misinformation, PR professionals must remain steadfast in their commitment to integrity and authenticity, safeguarding the credibility of the brands they represent.

Embracing Technology and Understanding Your Audience

As a veteran in the dynamic realm of PR in India, I have witnessed a remarkable transformation in the way we communicate, engage and influence. Today, adaptation isn't just a choice—it is a necessity for survival. So, what does the future hold for PR in the diverse and bustling landscape of India?

Technology and data have emerged as our trusted allies in this new era. Understanding our audience isn't just a guessing game anymore—it's a science that allows us to tailor our strategies with pinpoint precision. Thanks to advanced and sophisticated analytical tools, we can delve deep into the psyche of our target demography, uncovering insights that guide our decision-making process. AI is the silent force driving innovation in the business. From research and brainstorming to predictive analysis, AI has become an indispensable tool in our arsenal. Imagine having a virtual assistant that never sleeps, never tires and never misses a beat. By harnessing the power of AI for research, brainstorming, decision-making and content creation, we can unlock new levels of efficiency and creativity, propelling our profession forward into a bold new era of possibility.

In the era of big data and AI, brands can harness the power of personalisation to cut through the clutter and connect with their audience on a deeper, more meaningful level. Whether it is personalised email pitches, targeted social media campaigns or bespoke content recommendations, the future of PR lies in delivering the right message to the right person at the right time. When it comes to crisis management, in the digital age, news can escalate within minutes, spreading like wildfire across social networks and media outlets. PR professionals must have robust crisis communication plans in place by leveraging digital monitoring tools to identify emerging issues and engage with stakeholders in real time. In the future, crisis management will continue to be a critical skill set for PR professionals, requiring adaptability, resilience and strategic foresight in the face of adversity.

Of course, no discussion about the future of PR would be complete without mentioning the age-old art of storytelling. Whether we are crafting a press release, curating content for social media or pitching a story to journalists, storytelling remains at the heart of what we do. In the digital age, storytelling transcends traditional mediums and takes on new forms and formats. From immersive multimedia experiences to bite-sized social media snippets, the avenues are as diverse as they are dynamic.

Meanwhile, as public scrutiny intensifies and consumer expectations evolve, ethical communication has never been more important. In an age of fake news, misinformation and digital manipulation, PR professionals must respect the privacy and rights of individuals and take a stand on social and environmental issues that matter to our audience. This will go a long way in building long-term relationships with stakeholders and laying the foundation for sustainable success in the future.

In conclusion, the future of PR in India is bright, albeit challenging. We must continue to embrace change, harnessing the power of technology and storytelling to forge ahead with confidence, shaping the future of PR one story at a time.

17

Nikhil Khanna

Founder of Avian Media, currently Executive Chairman, Avian WE

'Fuelled by my passion for writing and media, I ventured to start out on my own, with early support from mentors.'

Transition from Advertising to Public Relations

I hail from Delhi and I graduated from the Sri Ram College of Commerce. I was raised in a family deeply rooted in chartered accountancy. The expectation loomed large for me to join the family firm, a legacy built by my grandfather and father from scratch—they had successfully established Khanna & Co. as one of India's leading CA firms. However, despite familial pressure, I soon realised that finance wasn't my forte.

I was introduced to the world of advertising by Mohammad Khan, where I found my niche as a copywriter. Subsequently, I became a pivotal part one of India's first PR firms, Good Relations, under the guidance of Ravi Dubey, eventually ascending to a directorial role after nine years.

Following a stint in content creation, ahead of its time but marred by the dot-com collapse, I learnt invaluable lessons from failure, emphasising prudent financial management and strategic partnerships. Fuelled by my passion for writing and media, I ventured to start Avian, with early support from mentors like Prema Sagar.

Deciding to expand beyond traditional PR, Avian diversified into public affairs, policy, digital, content and data, leveraging synergies for cross-selling opportunities. Recognising the importance of expertise, I surrounded myself with specialists in each vertical, fostering a culture of autonomy and support.

Seeking foreign investment, I forged partnerships with like-minded individuals from the West Coast of the United States, facilitating global expansion and integration. Today, with offices spanning continents, Avian stands as a testament to perseverance and strategic foresight.

Amidst the challenges, anecdotes abound, from makeshift office setups to memorable client interactions. Early endorsements from industry giants like Sona Steering and Airbus solidified Avian's reputation, paving the way for sustained growth and success.

No organisation can grow without a dream team. With Neha Mehrotra and Manash Neog that was, and is, that team. We were the first colleagues and remain so even today. And when Nitin Mantri came in as the CEO, all bets were resolutely on for growth and new heights!

In retrospect, each hurdle navigated and triumph celebrated has shaped the journey of Avian, underscoring the resilience and adaptability essential for entrepreneurial endeavours in the ever-evolving landscape of business and communication.

Then and Now

Then: It was hand-soapy and oleaginous.

Now: It's crisp, professional, to the point.

Then: It was delightfully vague.

Now: It's structured, focused and gimlet-eyed.

Then: It unfurled at five-star hotels featuring endless lunches fuelled by bottomless glasses.

Now: Lucky if you'll get a coffee. And rightly so. Who has the time anyway?

Then: A power sari lady or a smart-suited man with a posh accent from a public school was enough to make friends and influence people.

Now: People from small towns with a burning desire to succeed and build an enterprise are the stars. As the saying goes, 'No one cares, work hard.' And such people really work hard.

Then: Hierarchies flourished like great tropical jungles where 'workers' gingerly tapped the 'boss' (that word!), in archaic, hideously overdone offices. Think 'English' club chairs covered in cheap green pleather, heavy dark-brown furniture and cowering secretaries.

Now: The offices are bright, cheerful, noisy and vigorously open door. Light streams in, as do ideas.

Then: Clients were pudgy manufacturers of 'things' looking for 'inflooenze' in the dusty corridors of power via the media.

Now: Clients are vibrant and in smart, innovative industries that are both forward-looking new-techy.

Then: The media were either pompous old windbags with towering egos or ferrety chancers of the quiet make. Of course, there were the brilliant ones as well—too many to mention here, but suffice to say men and women who were journalists in the best traditions of the profession. Fearless, dedicated and inspired.

Now: The media—what's that?

Then: Social meant a cocktail party, and media was (see above).

Now: Social media is a monster that will grab, swallow and digest without even the slightest hint of an eructation.

'Change is the only constant,' said Heraclitus. He could have been speaking of the PR profession.

18

Nandita Lakshmanan

Founder and CEO of The PRactice

'We developed our skills through hands-on experience and a supportive environment. This self-starter attitude was a hallmark of our generation in the 1990s.'

News Anchor Dreams to a PR Firm

I HAVE INCREDIBLY VIVID MEMORIES OF MY CHILDHOOD, which almost always make me feel young. I grew up in Delhi, though I was born in Kottayam, Kerala, at my grandparents' place. After twenty-eight days, my family brought me back to Delhi, where I spent my formative years, including schooling, college and the start of my career at Genesis PR. I attended Apeejay School from third grade to twelfth grade. As an active student, I consistently performed well academically and participated in various extracurricular activities such as debates, declamations and sports, especially as a sprinter on the school team.

My father was a journalist who covered economics and politics during the 1970s and 1980s, a time when the media landscape was vastly different from today. Back then, there were only a few publications, and journalism was a very different field. It wasn't a business—it played the crucial role of the Fourth Estate. My father was a reclusive journalist, dedicated to his profession. In that era, platforms like Doordarshan had a select few journalists who were granted access to Parliament to cover proceedings and report on the daily news. My father had the accreditation to cover Parliament proceedings for Doordarshan and All India Radio.

My father changed jobs frequently, leading to some tough times for the family. Despite this, our home life prioritised good food, an environment that fostered independence and a plethora of books over material comforts. We didn't have a television until I was in the eleventh grade, which contributed to a frugal but fulfilling upbringing.

We lived in one of Delhi's first journalist colonies, which was a beautiful, gated community inspired by Swedish architecture. We moved there in 1978 when I was about eight or nine years old. Stability came from staying in the same locality and home for seventeen years, changing schools only once in my third grade and also changing jobs just once in my career—from Genesis to the firm I set up myself.

Growing up in a middle-class household with strong values, I saw my father prioritise principles over fast-paced career growth. He never really joined the rat race, and my mother resourcefully managed our limited finances. Her contentment and ability to make the most of what we had resulted in a happy childhood with a sense of abundance. I believe I have carried these lessons of loyalty, contentment and resourcefulness into my own life.

In school, everyone always pushed me to do more—teachers, fellow students, seniors. That's how I ended up participating in so many activities during my school years.

I prefer to be out of the spotlight, work at a pace comfortable to me. This makes many feel that I am not working to my full potential. To me, my space and peace of mind are important and I know what I can do well in twenty-four hours. Quite like my father, I will not be part of the rat race.

This experience influenced my decision to keep my business small. I wanted an organisation I could manage entirely on my own.

At eighteen, stepping out of home for the first time meant newfound independence and freedom. I chose Kamala Nehru College, which was not very far from home, just a few stops away by bus. My father believed in the concept of neighbourhood schools and therefore, it meant choosing a college that was close, so I could get time to pursue activities beyond academics. This proximity allowed me to pursue activities beyond college hours. I took up French and completed the Diplôme Supérieur, which took about four or five years. Additionally, I joined All India Radio (AIR) as a freelancer. AIR had a show called *Yuvavani*. *Yuvavani*, as the name suggested, was for the youth just out of school and in college, and everyone in Delhi aspired to host a segment called 'In the Groove', a half-hour slot where you were invited to the studio as the RJ to share your playlist with the listeners. This was a show I got to host. Eventually, I went on to become a regular announcer at Yuvavani.

During my undergraduate degree, I pursued an honours in English literature, followed by a master's in the same field. Concurrently, I worked as an announcer, although it wasn't a full-time job. These positions offered limited slots, maybe three to six days a month. The shifts were either from 5 a.m. to 8 a.m. or from 7 p.m. to 11 p.m.

Balancing part-time work and study was great. For morning shifts, I would leave home at 4 a.m., finish my shift and then head to college. For evening shifts, I would leave college by 5.30 p.m., go straight to the station, complete my slot and return home. I carried on with this even as I started my career, which meant I left home for my AIR shifts at 4.30 a.m. and got back only by 6.30 / 7 p.m., or if it was an evening shift, left home at 8 a.m. and got back at midnight.

I started earning at a young age. While in school and college, I tutored three students from my neighbourhood, making me one of the wealthier sixteen-year-olds. I saved my earnings to travel, even if it was just to Kerala, where my grandparents lived, by train, since flights were unaffordable.

These experiences made me fiercely independent. I continued teaching even while working. With my diploma in French, I also tutored neighbourhood children in the language. I loved teaching and had ambitions of being a Montessori teacher, but life had other plans for me.

I was enamoured by news reading, partly because we grew up with the radio instead of television, always tuned to international channels like the BBC. My father had a digital transistor, and I loved listening to it. Often, I would pretend to be a newsreader, reading out loud. Since my father was a journalist, we received eight newspapers daily. His day started with these newspapers, and I would join him in his room, reading alongside him.

My father taught us how to read a newspaper thoroughly, from the top left corner of the masthead to the bottom right of the back page. This method became a natural way for me to learn about the world. We read every section, from the front page to movie reviews, sports and comics. This practice instilled a deep understanding of current events and a love for reading.

Even in school, we were encouraged to be well-rounded and open-minded individuals. We read excerpts from various holy scriptures—Monday was the Ramayana, Tuesday the Mahabharata, Wednesday the Guru Granth Sahib and so on. Each morning, we read couplets. We also read the newspaper and wrote down the headlines. This habit was ingrained in us from childhood.

Journalism would have been my backup plan, specifically news reading. I dreamed of being an anchor on a news channel or an RJ, using my voice to connect with others. But here I am, running a PR firm instead.

Initially, I planned to continue my academic journey with a master's, then an MPhil, and eventually a PhD. I thought the academic route would be easier than the professional one. However, I met a college mate on the road one day. She was working with *City Guide* and had joined as an editor. She told me her boss was setting up a PR firm and asked if I was interested in a job.

At that point, I also auditioned for Delhi B at AIR, which was a promotion of sorts from my earlier role at *Yuvavani* because it was a national channel. During this time, I also operated India's first ever FM studio and did voiceovers to make a living! I finally auditioned for news reading at AIR, qualified and then gave it up to move to Bangalore to set up Genesis' first ever office outside Delhi.

My sister had joined Corporate Voice in Bangalore in 1991 or 1992. She had sent me a *Business Today* article about the emerging PR profession, featuring pioneers like Dilip Cherian, Rajiv Desai, Ravi Dubey and Prema Sagar. The profession seemed intriguing as it combined journalism and desk work, so I decided to give it a try.

Two days after reading the article, I met my college roommate Sanjana again. She set up an interview with Prema for me, and despite knowing nothing about the profession, I got the job. I interviewed in February or March and joined on 23 May 1993, with a salary of ₹2,200 as a junior account executive. I was in my early twenties at that time.

I quickly fell in love with the job. The environment at Genesis was incredibly welcoming, and it felt like a perfect fit for me.

My father was taken aback when I told him about my new job. When I mentioned it was in PR, he grimaced. As a journalist, he had often been hounded by PR professionals, and we grew up lying to the PR professionals, saying he wasn't home or had just left for the office. The thought of his daughter doing the same thing was shocking to him. However, once he understood what my work actually entailed, he found it fascinating.

My first clients were India Habitat Centre and a small travel company owned by ITC called Travel House. I led the launch of the Habitat Centre, my first assignment. Prema and Gita Singh were involved, but there was no team, just me. I had to produce the first stakeholder newsletter for the India Habitat Centre, creating the layout and writing it by hand, as we had only one computer. Everything, from selecting paper to designing the newsletter, was done manually.

My role involved extensive media relations, which I dreaded at first. However, I had an amazing coach in Archana Jain, and Prema's principles were invaluable. She had just returned from Europe after studying at the Frank Jefkins School of Public Relations in the UK, bringing textbook PR knowledge to us. Even today, I'm a big proponent of the academic definitions of PR.

We were exposed to a comprehensive understanding of earning respect as PR professionals, the value we bring to clients, and how research and reading can enhance our work. We began our days by reading newspapers, cutting and pasting articles onto paper and making notes.

One of the tasks assigned to me was building Genesis' first media database. I manually keyed in every entry from the INS directory, a massive book listing media contacts and circulation figures. This task, which involved hours of data entry, was a labour of love for me. Growing up with a typewriter at home and learning typing and shorthand in the tenth grade, I was thrilled to use a computer keyboard.

This exercise helped me learn much about the media landscape, as I meticulously entered every detail. The immersive activity burnt all the media contacts across the country into my memory. The experience was invaluable and formative in my early career.

We were very conscious of getting things right the first time. Everything had to be perfect on the first try. Prema, with her beautiful handwriting and a sharpened pencil, would meticulously edit all our press releases. These memories are incredibly precious to me, as they represent a time of learning from the best in the profession.

Two significant things led to my move to Bangalore. First, I had always loved Bangalore, having visited often due to family living there. Second, Prema mentioned in a conversation that Genesis was ready to set up an office outside Delhi, and Bangalore seemed ideal given my family connections. Around the same time, my parents were starting to realise they had a somewhat moody and rebellious twenty-three-year-old at home, and they were on the verge of suggesting I find my own place. These factors aligned perfectly, so I packed my bags and left. I had spent about a year and a half at Genesis in Delhi, from 1993 to early 1995.

I moved to Bangalore in February 1995 with just a suitcase. I remember Prema and I driving around Bangalore to find an apartment that could serve as both my home and office. We found a beautiful two-bedroom apartment with coconut tree leaves leaning into the balcony. One bedroom became my office, and the other was my living space. We shipped all necessary furniture and equipment, including fax machines, to Bangalore, and I set everything up. I still have some pieces of that furniture and a collection of beautifully bound *Reader's Digest* volumes.

At that time, KFC was a client of Genesis, and they were launching their first restaurant in Bangalore on Brigade Road amidst a storm of controversy. A self-styled activist was leading the protests against it, and the MSG crisis also erupted around that time in 1995. The MSG levels in KFC were said to be too high.

It was a challenging time. The issue was that 0.02 per cent of MSG was allowed in food, but there was no clear, transparent information about it. Activists seized on this lack of transparency, but we had ample evidence to refute their claims, showing that KFC was well within the permissible limits. Despite the restaurant being stormed by activists, we persevered.

I was in Bangalore, coordinating closely with Prema, Archana and the rest of team. We finally managed to launch the restaurant amidst the chaos. It was a trial by fire for me, handling a crisis of this magnitude, while being by myself in the city, even as I received guidance from the best. The experience was invaluable, teaching me a great deal and instilling in me a sense of fearlessness. I approached the situation solely focusing on what needed to be done, and not thinking about the outcome. And that's a lesson I carry with me—just do one's best transparently, factually; the outcomes will follow. Also, in a crisis, clamming up is never a solution. Be bold, put out the facts and counter half-baked opinions.

This mindset brought its own rewards and joy. As a young professional managing such a significant crisis, I earned a lot of respect and built strong relationships with journalists. For the first time, a PR firm was providing factual, timely information and being responsible and accessible, which made life easier for the media. It was a new and positive experience for them, engaging with a PR firm in such a constructive manner during a crisis. That year was truly formative and rewarding.

I remember getting my first mobile phone when I moved to Bangalore, around 1995 or 1996. Before that, we relied on landline calls, and we had only one computer and a dot matrix printer, which made that terrible noise while printing.

I worked at Genesis until September 1999. After resigning, I spent a few months exploring what I could do next, considering roles like joining corporate communications, but nothing seemed to fit. My then-husband suggested I start my own venture. Around this time, I received an opportunity from Acer India, which was setting up a 100 per cent subsidiary in India and breaking away from Wipro. Bharat Gopalakrishnan, who has since passed away, reached out to me about joining them as a consultant. It was an early-stage setup, so I found myself working closely with senior management at Acer India, managing their PR machinery.

This experience inspired me to establish my own firm. I started taking on consulting assignments, and as demand grew, I formalised my business in 2000.

My first client was Acer India, not Infosys, as many believe. I also worked with Grey Cell Technologies, represented as Unimobile, led by the poster boy of start-ups and product technology, Rajesh Reddy. Rajesh was a serial entrepreneur, and we continued working with him on his next venture, July Systems. Another early client was an eCRM company called TriVium Systems. These were small accounts, but I cherished them, valuing the relationships and respect we built. When Infosys came on board, I remember the pivotal moment clearly. It was another significant milestone, but my journey up to that point was filled with rich experiences that prepared me for the challenges and opportunities ahead.

Somashekar (who continues to be my assistant today), Anupama Menon and Kadambari Gopinath were the first three employees at The PRactice.

At thirty years, I was leading a team of young professionals in their early twenties. From Genesis, I had learnt that age was no barrier to earning respect or being a star performer, if you conducted yourself with professionalism and integrity. We didn't rely on extensive training programmes. Instead, we developed our skills through hands-on experience and a supportive environment. This self-starter attitude was a hallmark of our generation in the 1990s. I saw that in my colleagues who were launching their careers or still in the very early stages—they were resourceful and mature self-starters and thorough professionals.

Today, it seems every skill requires formal training, creating a sense of entitlement and dependency. The current generation is inundated with platitudes on LinkedIn and other social media platforms, which doesn't foster the same level of self-reliance and initiative. Reflecting on my journey, I appreciate the invaluable lessons from Genesis that shaped my approach to leadership and client relationships.

It is difficult to have one memorable campaign in a career that spans over three decades. But multi-stakeholder work that aligns to the full potential of PR and business objectives is what excites and challenges me. The launch of Terminal 1, Bangalore International Airport (today KIAL) amidst controversy back in 2009, was one such assignment. There was white-collar activism, lack of government support and a massive misinformation and disinformation campaign that weighed against them. Yet again, sticking to facts, with transparency and unwavering commitment to presenting the truth, we won over the media and other influencers.

Spending a sleepless night at the airport on the day of the launch, welcoming the first flight, pre-empting issues with the airport processes, combatting a vitiated stakeholder environment—these memories come alive each time I fly through one of India's, and perhaps the world's, most functional airports.

The Continuous Rise of PR

Not so long ago, in the last decade of the twentieth century, PR was defined by its comprehensive approach, articulated by Frank Jefkins as 'the planned and sustained effort to establish and maintain goodwill and mutual understanding between an organisation and its publics'. These 'publics' encompassed a wide spectrum of stakeholders including employees, government entities, civil society organisations, customers, partners and suppliers.

The landscape in the last two decades has undergone profound changes. The turn of the century saw not only the rise of technology giants, heightened stereotyping of millennials and Gen Z as consumers and in the workforce, but also geopolitics making its presence felt like never before. And of course, COVID-19 upended our lives. Today, with social media and advanced analytics tools, we can gauge stakeholder sentiment in real time, accelerating communication, but paradoxically, leaving several brands out of touch with on-ground reality.

Storytelling holds centre stage among PR practitioners today. The focus is narrowly on last-mile communications with the intent to reach stakeholders via social media, digital campaigns and influencer partnerships, and the waning print and television media. From the time when media relations once meant earned visibility, it is not uncommon to hear RFPs (requests for proposal) and client briefs speak of the ESOP model (earned, shared, owned and paid).

This shift from stakeholder engagement to last-mile communication has led to the rise of distinct functions like public policy practitioners, CSR specialists, analyst relations firms—all of whom have taken a slice of PR to build capacities and capabilities to emerge as industries in themselves. Further, the media landscape has transformed dramatically, with traditional outlets like newspapers and TV being supplemented by digital platforms and social networks. Individuals and organisations can now influence public discourse directly, challenging the relevance of myopic media relations strategies.

Globalisation, once a unifying force, now presents challenges as nationalist sentiments and geopolitical tensions reshape dynamics. PR practitioners, across sectors, must navigate this complex terrain, adapting strategies to diverse cultural and political contexts. The rise of misinformation further complicates efforts, necessitating vigilance in safeguarding credibility and reputation.

It is therefore interesting that the fundamentals of PR practice hold true today, even as communication channels have evolved. While technology enhances targeted communications, it prompts a reassessment of the focus on stakeholder engagement. The emergence of specialisation and the decoupling of essential stakeholder functions has fragmented responsibilities, risking a loss of cohesive focus on fostering goodwill across all stakeholders.

There are distinct signs of progress. In the last few years, Indian PR stalwarts have put India on the global map, helming prominent international associations like the International Communications Consultancy Organisation (ICCO) and International Association for Measurement and Evaluation of Communication (AMEC) and taking on international roles. The number of institutes offering professional and vocational degrees in PR is on the rise, and the day is not far when educational institutions recognising the transdisciplinary nature of PR will promote it as they do management courses.

The Future is Ours to Keep

The world is undeniably in flux. With over fifty elections taking place globally in 2024, the urgency to meet Sustainable Development Goals (SDGs) by 2030, and the escalating climate crisis, among other challenges, the stakes have never been higher. Besides, the nature of jobs and expectations from leaders across organisations and institutions are changing. In this lies the opportunity for PR practitioners to balance applications of technology with foundational principles of stakeholder engagement, making PR indispensable to organisations and institutions.

We will face unprecedented ethical dilemmas in the next decade. With ethics, transparency and trust-building underpinning the very premise of PR, there is potential for us to drive critical conversations and shape the world into a better place. This is a tall order, and it calls for a complete upheaval in our thinking as merely last-mile communicators.

PR views every opportunity and challenge from a 360-degree lens. This is because we (ideally) keep stakeholders at the centre of decisions, an imperative to navigate twenty-first-century market realities. If I were to predict the future of our profession, I would paint a blank canvas, for the existing reputation of our profession may be somewhat muddied, confused and limiting.

The future is promising, but it requires a shift in our own mindset and a decision to lead, not be led by perceptions of what PR means and does. A few predictions:

- PR will be recognised and sought after as a management discipline and will emerge as the new management philosophy / principle. A new language for PR, which is assertive, critical and transdisciplinary, will emerge.
- Increased deep research in the field will produce frameworks and models that are evidence-based, impact-oriented and multi-stakeholder in approach.
- Practitioners and thinkers who bring serious and independent points of view to the forefront will be considered voices of reason in a profession in intense flux. They will join hands and create think tanks, be more involved in the policy-making process and lend their expertise to decision-making at the highest levels. This

new breed of fierce and deep thinkers will be modern-day ethicists.

- More PR practitioners will move into management roles, leading organisations and institutions as CEOs. Brazen profiteering will no longer be the norm as a new world order emerges. This is both an opportunity and a challenge.
- Technology will continue to evolve. The use of data with precision and ethical behaviour will be sought after, and advice will be sought on deeper matters of closing the gap between perception and reality.

The future of PR is one of adaptability and leading from the front. By staying true to the core principles of stakeholder engagement, embracing technological advancements and committing to ethical practices, PR can emerge from the shadows of ambiguity and irrelevance. The goal is to build a better future, one where businesses and institutions act as stewards of trust and agents of positive change. The challenge is significant, but with investment and a change in our own mindset, the future is ours to keep.

19

Gaurav Patra

Joint Group COO and Co-Founder of V360 Group

'Reading is akin to earning a master's degree in PR or journalism, as it enriches one's knowledge base and sharpens their skills for navigating the complexities of communication in today's world.'

From Journalism to Public Relations

I was born in Cuttack into a family of doctors. Both my parents have their own practice there, and my older brother is also a doctor. I completed my schooling from Odisha, attending a government school, and then pursued my graduation and post-graduation at Ravenshaw College, a prestigious institution in Odisha with over 150 years of history. Following my post-graduation, I earned a journalism degree from the Indian Institute of Mass Communication.

My professional journey began in 1994 with my first job at Cyber Media, where I worked for the magazine *Voice and Data*. I spent around twelve years as a journalist, my journalism career culminating at *The Indian Express* in their business publication division. There, I served as assistant bureau chief, managing the *Express Computer* magazine in Delhi. I remained in journalism until 2005.

Despite enjoying journalism, I was always drawn to PR, having studied it as part of my coursework. However, I struggled to find the right opportunities in PR initially. I gave interviews and received offers from consultancies, but for various reasons, I didn't join them at the time.

In 2005, my wife, Meenakshi Mohanty, suggested that I start my own business, something related to my profession. She believed I had built a strong network and had valuable contacts from my years in journalism. This idea resonated with me, and I decided to venture into PR on my own. Before founding Value 360 Communications, I had started another company, but the partnership didn't work out.

In 2007, I teamed up with Kunal Sinha and Manisha Chaudhary to start Value 360 Communications. Kunal and I knew each other from our previous interactions. He used to visit me when I was a journalist, while he was working with a PR firm. I found him to be a very pleasant and capable person. Recognising his expertise in PR, I approached him with the idea of starting our own firm. With Kunal's and Manisha's experience in PR and my background in journalism, we combined our strengths to build Value 360 Communications.

We started off in South Extension in Delhi with a small, two-room office. After some time, we moved to Sant Nagar. Initially, we had just one floor there, but as we grew, we expanded to two, three, four and eventually five floors. Just before COVID-19, we relocated to our new office in Okhla. Now, we have two offices in the city: one for Value 360 and another for sister brands PopKorn and ClanConnect, which operate from the other building. Initially, being new to the business, it was challenging to attract good-quality employees. However, we were fortunate to have had some bright and talented individuals join our team.

As a journalist, I had established connections with many clients. When we started, I reached out to these contacts, and a few of them agreed to sign us up. That's how we got our initial clients and got the business off the ground. Our first client was The Siemon Company, a cabling client. I'm not sure if they're still in India, but they were one of the first to sign with us. It was a very small client, but that's how we got our start.

Currently, we serve over 200 clients, and our team has grown to over 250 employees. We operate from multiple offices across the country, apart from the offices in Delhi.

During that time, the start-up spirit was thriving, and there was a surge in technological advancements. This environment provided fertile ground for our growth and development.

Securing Snapdeal as one of our first major clients, despite the dynamic nature of the start-up realm, facilitated our rapid growth and expansion within the industry. Snapdeal started off as a smaller player, but through our collaboration, we executed some remarkable campaigns that contributed significantly to our growth. Our strategic focus extended beyond start-ups, encompassing the technology, education and hospitality sectors, further diversifying our portfolio and solidifying our position in the market.

We have had the privilege of collaborating with numerous unicorns. Our extensive client roster includes many prominent names, reflecting our strong presence and successful partnerships within the start-up ecosystem.

For newcomers in PR, developing a habit of regularly reading newspapers and magazines is foundational. It not only keeps them informed about current affairs and industry trends but also helps them understand the evolving dynamics of the media landscape. As they progress in their careers, this habit remains invaluable, guiding them in suggesting story ideas, understanding the trajectory of the field and honing their expertise in PR or journalism. Indeed, reading is akin to earning a master's degree in PR or journalism, as it enriches one's knowledge base and sharpens their skills for navigating the complexities of communication in today's world.

Over the years, we have done some memorable work for ONDC, PayTM, MG Motors and Audi, to name a few. These campaigns have gone on to win several awards.

Evolution from Press Releases to Digital Influencers

The evolution of PR in India over the last twenty years has been profound. It has transitioned from traditional press-centric tactics to a sophisticated, multi-channel approach that leverages technology to create meaningful connections and build lasting relationships with stakeholders.

Back in the early 2000s, PR in India was predominantly about media relations, press releases and event management. The focus was on print and broadcast media as the primary channels for disseminating information and shaping public opinion. The role of PR was more reactive than proactive, often limited to damage control during crises.

The turning point came with the advent of the internet and social media. The mid-2000s saw the rise of digital platforms, which began to change the way PR campaigns were executed. There was a shift towards more engaging, two-way communication, allowing real-time interaction with audiences. The digital era also brought about a need for content that was not just informative but also shareable and visually appealing.

The last decade in particular has seen a significant shift towards data-driven PR. Analytics and metrics have become crucial in understanding audience behaviour, campaign performance and ROI. The ability to track and measure the impact of PR activities has led to more strategic and targeted campaigns.

Moreover, the role of PR has expanded beyond media relations to include influencer engagement, content marketing and reputation management. PR professionals are now expected to be adept at storytelling, brand building and crisis management across multiple platforms.

The PR landscape today is dynamic and complex. It requires a deep understanding of cultural nuances, regional diversity and the ever-changing media ecosystem. As we move forward, the integration of artificial intelligence and machine learning is set to further revolutionise the business, making it more personalised and predictive.

Traditional Practices and Innovative Technologies

To me, the future of PR appears to be an exciting amalgamation of traditional practices and innovative technologies. PR has gone from being a primarily media-centric profession to a more dynamic one that encompasses a wide array of communication strategies. The integration of PR with marketing is becoming increasingly seamless, leading to a comprehensive approach to brand communication. This convergence is not just about managing reputations but also about actively contributing to business growth through lead generation and sales.

The digital realm, particularly social media, is set to dominate PR strategies. These platforms have become the primary channels for storytelling, crisis management and consumer engagement. The rise of short-form video content and interactive features demands that PR professionals create compelling visual narratives that resonate with their audiences. Moreover, the use of analytics and big data will become indispensable in crafting effective PR campaigns. Professionals will rely on data to tailor their campaigns, measure their impact and understand audience behaviour, necessitating a stronger focus on research and analytical skills within the business.

Personalisation is another trend that is shaping the future of PR. Audiences are increasingly seeking personalised experiences, and PR campaigns will need to cater to individual preferences and behaviours. This will involve leveraging AI and machine learning to deliver targeted content and build deeper connections with stakeholders. Moreover, with a growing emphasis on CSR, PR will play a crucial role in promoting ethical practices and sustainability. Transparent and authentic communication will be paramount in building trust with the public.

As businesses expand globally, PR professionals will need to navigate cross-cultural communication while also localising content to resonate with regional audiences. Understanding diverse markets and adapting messages accordingly will be essential. Furthermore, emerging technologies like virtual reality, augmented reality and blockchain will open up new avenues for PR, offering immersive experiences and enhancing the credibility of communication. As PR professionals, we must evolve to remain relevant and effective in this dynamic setting, ensuring that our strategies are not only innovative but also ethically sound and culturally sensitive.

20

Roger C.B. Pereira

Founder of Roger Pereira Communications LLP

'The highlight of my career was working on the Green Revolution, the White Revolution and also with Prime Minister Indira Gandhi and JRD Tata.'

From Ranwar Village to the Global Stage

I come from a village in Mumbai called Ranwar near Bandra, where I grew up. As a child, I was short and chubby, but very bold and outspoken. Bandra felt like one big village where religion and caste didn't matter—we were all like family. I attended St Stanislaus School and later went to St Xavier's College. Post my graduation, I joined the Government Law College and the University Department of Political Science to pursue my master's degree.

I started my career in communications at the age of seventeen, participating in radio plays thanks to Adi Marzban and Bubbles Padamsee, along with voicing / writing scripts for the Films Division. I was in my second year of college, then. My college mate Partap Sharma introduced me to the Films Division, which needed new voices. This involved doing the commentary for Indian news reels and documentaries by the Films Division. Later, this expanded into writing these commentaries too. That was my introduction to media.

Originally, I thought I would be an actor. I was very much into theatre. Ebrahim Alkazi, who later founded the National School of Drama, was commissioned by Prithviraj Kapoor to coach his son, Shashi Kapoor. Since Prithviraj was funding the entire programme, I was asked if I would act opposite Shashi Kapoor for a token ₹10 per month. I was thrilled. Joy Mukherjee, a classmate at St Xavier's, got to know about this. He asked if he could join too! With his father, a producer, it would help him get into movies. Those were the days!

While in college, I had also joined the NCC Air Wing. In my third year, I had the opportunity to learn flying. I started seriously considering joining the Indian Air Force. On completing four years with the NCC Air Wing, I could get a direct entry into the Indian Air Force. My parents were unaware of my plans until the eve of my interview. At that time too, there were border skirmishes. No sooner had my parents gotten to know about the purpose of my visit to Dehradun that I received a telegram instructing me to return home immediately.

I had no Plan B. A family friend, Dr Aloo Dastur and the legendary Dr Usha Mehta, who led the Department of Political Science of the University of Bombay, suggested that I should pursue my master's in political science. Since the courses were in the afternoon, I joined the morning sessions of the Government Law College. However, the big question still hung over my head: what next?

Alkazi suggested I try advertising. He was the creative director at Shilpi at the time. Advertising seemed a good option for many associated with the Bombay stage. There was Gerson da Cunha, Alyque Padamsee and many more who were active in both fields. So off I went to Shilpi for a copy test. I failed. I tried a few other advertising agencies. The same result. The truth was, I wasn't a writer!

Then one day, I happened to meet the newly promoted copy chief of J. Walter Thompson, Noel Godin, at a hair-cutting salon. We had acted together in a couple of plays. He inquired what I was doing besides college and plays. I updated him about my situation, and he invited me to his office. Instead of the traditional writing test, he created a test to assess my creativity. He offered me a job immediately. I had just turned twenty. The rest is history.

While at JWT, I had the opportunity to get acquainted with that mountain of a human being and India's leading industrialist, J.R.D. Tata, who was the chairman of Air India at that time. JWT created ads for Air India, among many other clients. I believe my flying experience did give me an advantage there. That acquaintance blossomed into mentorship that eventually inspired and guided me into setting up a PR consultancy in April 1987 with Tata Sons as my first client! More on this later.

In 1965, by sheer accident, I was the recipient of a Global Advertising Award by the International Advertising Association in New York, which catapulted me into prominence at just twenty-four.

Our country was forced into defending our borders. Razmi Ahmed of Lintas and Premnarayan Indernarayan of Sistas volunteered the services of the Advertising Agencies Association of India (AAAI) to help the Ministry of Information & Broadcasting led by Mrs Indira Gandhi. A three-member team from different agencies was formed to prepare a campaign to communicate our story. There was a perception, at that time, that we were losing the battle. Jit Kantawala, the leader of the team, made the presentation to Mrs Gandhi. She seemed unimpressed. After a detailed discussion with the three of us, Mrs Gandhi inquired why there wasn't a PR strategy in our approach. She then asked me pointedly if I knew PR. I admitted my ignorance and inexperience of that discipline. She asked if I was willing to learn. I readily agreed. I was requested to stay on, and Prasanto Sanyal, a PR veteran from Indian Oxygen, Calcutta, was requisitioned to mentor me for the task at hand. I learnt from the best! India eventually won the war.

Following the war, there was a food shortage, and Mrs Gandhi's team requested me to stay on and help with a motivational campaign to convince farmers to use hybrid seeds. It was a great experience. I had the opportunity to work on both the Green Revolution and the White Revolution.

Incidentally, I joined Shilpi on the insistence of another legend who had a great influence on me, Dr Vikram Sarabhai. This was in March 1963. The same Shilpi that turned me down in 1959! I worked with this organisation till November 1985. I had given notice of my intended departure on 1 January1980. The group that had been painstakingly built by Vikram Sarabhai was going downhill. I gave notice that unless things changed, I didn't wish to be buried in the debris. The change was only for the worse. So, I left in November 1985.

I had a terrific career at Shilpi, where we executed some fabulous campaigns. The creation and launch of ENERGEE for the Government of Maharashtra was one. Another was our entrepreneurial development campaign for the Government of Gujarat, a project close to my heart as I spent a significant amount of time (1972–85) there. It was so successful that we were invited by the then Andhra Pradesh Chief Minister

N.T. Rama Rao and the then Punjab Chief Minister Darbara Singh to replicate the campaigns in their respective states.

It all started in 1972, when I met Manubhai Shah, the then Union Minister for Commerce, on a flight from Delhi to Ahmedabad. He began inquiring about my work and the field of advertising. He then asked if I could create a campaign to attract Gujarati businessmen back to Gujarat from Maharashtra. This led to the launch of the 'Invest in Gujarat' campaign, which was a tremendous success and continues to run in Gujarat to this day in different avatars.

For all our campaigns, we used both PR and advertising, one complementing the other. Sometimes using advertising to communicate what would normally be executed through PR. The experience in Delhi in 1965 came in handy ever since! While at Shilpi, I had the opportunity of meeting another nation builder: Dr Verghese Kurien. For the National Dairy Development Board (NDDB), our work was entirely PR-focused in the villages, amongst cooperatives. I must have got malaria some seven or eight times! So much so, I became immune to the malaria medication. The work gave me immense satisfaction though. I continued to work for NDDB and the Institute of Rural Management Anand (IRMA) even after I left Shilpi. That was the one exception to the norm.

I was finally relieved from Shilpi in 1985 with the condition that I shouldn't work in advertising or take Shilpi's clients or staff. I had no idea what I would do next, but my experience in advertising had involved a lot of PR work, including numerous IPOs. I needed to leave so I agreed to the terms.

I was offered a lot of consulting projects courtesy of my long-time friend, Bapu Deolalikar, who left the group for similar reasons several years prior and settled in Washington. I joined Bapu on my first assignment in Indonesia, focusing on nutrition and family planning. I continued to receive assignments in Washington, Japan, Yemen, etc.

Then one day, I received a call from my very first mentor: J.R.D. Tata. He inquired about the work I was doing. I told him I would like to produce a TV serial on issues concerning women. He agreed to fund it and sponsor the fifty-two-episode serial: *Humraahi*. It was a great success. It won several awards and generated a lot of interest and inquiries from viewers. Mr Tata suggested I start an advertising agency. I told him about my non-compete agreement. I also shared the fact that several global advertising agencies like Young & Rubicam, Grey, etc. had offered to collaborate with me. Then Jeh, as he suggested I address him, advised I start a PR consultancy, which could also use advertising as they had done for TISCO, now Tata Steel. I jumped at the suggestion. He immediately offered Tata Sons and several Tata businesses as my initial clients. He also recommended us to Sushim Datta, then chairman of Hindustan Unilever Limited (HUL). (Tata were selling TOMCO and Lakme to HUL). And that's how it all began.

Originally, the firm was named Roger Pereira Consultants, to enable receiving some tax concessions available at that time to professionals transitioning to entrepreneurship. Later, we rebranded it as Roger Pereira Communications.

Our relationship with Burson-Marsteller began as an affiliate through Young & Rubicam, their parent. The legendary Harold Burson and I became very close collaborators. In the early 2000s, the Y & R Group was bought over by WPP. Then, Edelman reached out to us, and we joined hands with them. The time was ripe. The Indian market had just opened, and we had the honour and privilege of handling the market entries of virtually every major multinational. Some, like Mercedes

Benz, came to us for their relaunch. We continued to grow our domestic clientele too. In 2009, on reaching the age of seventy, I decided to retire and focus on giving back. And that's what I do even in 2024! My global partners tried to convince me to work part time either from Mumbai or New York. I had several options. But my mind was made. I stood firm. And in 2024, I have no regrets! Just mental satisfaction!

The Evolution of PR is Steeped in History

Let me tell it like it was. And perhaps, will be ...!

My first interaction with the communication profession was in the early 1950s. The company we now call Bharat Petroleum was then known as Burmah Shell. This company ran an advertising campaign: 'In India's life and part of it!'. As a twelve-year-old, I was intrigued. We had just won our independence. This company was seemingly British. It had another country's name—Burmah. Why the 'h' in the spelling? I couldn't figure out! And to add to my confusion, more and more Brits were leaving the country. Some were even selling off their companies. So how could a Brit company with another country's name claim to be in India's life and part of it after we had won our independence?

Then, one day I happened to meet Mr M.M. Roy, who worked closely with the legendary Mr Rose who headed the PR department. This campaign was to counter nationalisation. He explained as best he could to a twelve-year-old that advertising was part of PR and that the advertising department worked with D.J. Keymers, who in turn created advertisements based on themes developed by the PR department. Roy put me on their mailing list. The result was that I was the recipient of a series of booklets on that theme.

I believe StanVac and Caltex had similar models. So did Air India. Except that Air India had its own studio that produced posters, sales letters and so on for their offices worldwide. All under the PR department led by Jal Cowasjee, who also had PR managers (like my college mate Ramesh Sattawalla) reporting to him. The Tata Group too had a similar setup with Farrokh Mulla leading the PR portfolio. He reported to Sharoukh Sabavala, as did all the advertising leaders in each company, and was under the overall control of a member of the board. Almost all the other business groups followed the same model. To conclude, PR kept holding the leadership position.

I guess it was sometime in the late 1950s that advertising started getting more visible. In my humble opinion, the credit goes to Air India advertising, followed by AMUL advertising. Then, there was the Taj Hotels campaign. Air India was, for a long time, the preferred brand for customers, chosen over virtually all global brands! To my mind, at that time, this was the only Indian brand to get this preferential treatment.

It is my belief that advertising took the driver's seat primarily because it could be attributable to the creators. However, PR continued to be anonymous. This continued so long as the press (as in the printed media) dominated the media scene.

This was when I joined advertising on 1 December 1960. There were PR gurus then like Rudy Von Leyden and Victor Paranjyoti, among others, but these icons shot into prominence more because of their extracurricular work than their profession. Advertising seemed to have many more such mavericks: apart from Gerson da Cunha and Alyque Padamsee, there was Kersey Katrak, Panna Jain, Subhash Ghoshal, Arun Kolhatkar and a whole list of names I could fill pages and pages with. So, advertising took centre stage and the leadership. With each decade, newer names kept emerging in the advertising industry. PR on the other hand began to play second fiddle to advertising. Then came the time when PR started employing advertising. The most memorable campaign was the one for TISCO (Tata Steel) entitled 'We also make steel'. This was in the late 1970s, when the company was threatened with nationalisation!

Then came TV in the 1970s. And soon, thanks to Vasant Sathe (the then union minister for information and broadcasting), colour TV in the 1980s. Press advertising got competition. It fought back. But in the process, the star factor began to diminish. Then digital media started emerging in the early 2000s. Then in 2020 came the lockdown. And the press, barring a few exceptions, seems to have lost its prima donna status.

The Future Will be Glorious!

PR has come a long way. I see digital media taking the front seat. I see a closer relationship between PR and advertising. In fact, the line separating the two will gradually fade. This raises two questions: will there be advertising agencies? And will there be PR firms? It is my belief that there will be communication consultancies. And gradually, these will merge with consulting firms like McKinsey, PWC, EY and the likes. Time will tell.

21

Bela Rajan

Co-Founder of Sampark PR (later Ketchum Sampark), currently Director, August One Partners LLP

'The journey from being an individual practitioner to leading a consultancy with over 150 clients was beyond anything I had ever dreamt of.'

Banking to PR

I was born in a small town in North Gujarat called Visnagar. My father was the first amongst his siblings to move to Mumbai for further studies before Independence. Professionally, he was a sales and marketing person and was a socialist who believed in gender parity in those days.

In the days when a girl child was not so welcome, I remember my mother telling me that my father was so thrilled when I was born that he distributed sweets to all. I attended Fatima Devi English High School in Malad and later majored in psychology at Jai Hind College in Churchgate.

My journey into PR wasn't planned. During my early years, I dreamt of becoming a teacher, but I soon outgrew those aspirations. I then set my sights on becoming a lawyer. After completing a post-graduation in law, I joined a law firm but soon realised my heart was not in it.

I then had a stint with a cooperative bank—Rajan (who I later married) was a colleague there briefly—and then I moved to an export house. While I was working at these places, I also completed a course in advertising and journalism from KC College.

I learnt from a friend that the ninth PR World Congress was to be hosted in India. This was in the early 1980s. I seized the opportunity to work as the coordinator in the newly set-up secretariat for the executive committee of the congress. Though the conference was only three days, the preparation and marketing work began almost a year in advance. This stint taught me the importance of planning, teamwork, delegation of responsibilities and networking.

I was truly awestruck by the PR, marketing and advertising stalwarts, whom I met during that time and dealt with closely.

Thanks to my exposure, after the conference, I received numerous job offers from corporates and consultancies and finally chose to join one of India's first pure PR consultancies, Consilium Pvt. Ltd. The consultancy was handling several notable clients, such as Union Carbide, SKF Bearing, Atlas Copco, Boeing and World Trade Centre, among others. Consilium was a boutique firm largely handling multinationals and large Indian corporates, and the varied exposure I received during my stint held me in good stead not only in my next corporate assignment but also when I set up my consultancy.

After a few years with Consilium, I joined a large engineering company as their communications manager.

Meanwhile, the pressure to get married was building up from my family, so Rajan and I decided to tie the knot some months after my joining the engineering firm. Life became a roller coaster when our twin boys arrived, and I had to quit my job and take a sabbatical.

Once the kids became a year old, I took up freelance PR assignments apart from editing corporate house journals. I was also selected to edit *Solus*, the monthly magazine of the Advertising Club of Bombay.

While working on the ninth PR World Conference, I had noticed that every press release ended with the phrase 'Sampark karo'. When translated from Hindi, this phrase, meaning 'connect / get in touch', resonated with me, and that's how I chose 'Sampark' as the name of my firm. Of course, the name consistently evoked a mixed response. Some people loved it; some thought it was too Indian!

My first client when I resumed work after my sabbatical was SKF Bearings, and then others like ABB followed. I also serviced the PR requirements of clients of Aquarius Multimedia, an ad agency. I continued to work part time, tending to the children in the morning and working in the afternoon. The PR assignments started growing over the next few years, and I had eight or ten regular projects and retainer clients.

Around this time, Rajan too quit his job with Essar and decided to take the plunge and join me in making Sampark a larger firm. On 1 August 1994, we reinvented Sampark in its new avatar as a private limited company.

On the day we commenced Sampark in a corporatised set up, we had about twelve or fifteen clients. The challenge was more in getting good people to manage these clients. We were also fortunate that several big corporates were willing to sign us up for long-term engagements (three to five years) and were even willing to pay us signing fees!

I continued to spend the latter half of my day working, as my children were still young and needed me.

While Rajan handled the business and many of the clients, I largely took care of the consumer and brand clients besides key media relationships. I also oversaw the HR, accounts and administration functions of the firm.

While we were not credited as a brand partner, I am really proud of a huge innovation we came up as a team for ITC, for which we handled all corporate, brands and sponsorships. While managing the PR for sports sponsorship by their various brands, we found that in the event photo coverage the next day, the brand logo was often truncated. ITC had a stringent evaluation criterion for measuring our efficacy for event PR. We found that we often lost marks for photo coverage, as the brand was not fully visible. After a lot of brainstorming, our team came up with the innovative idea of a backdrop with the brand logo in a grid format, and this way we ensured that in any subsequent event coverage, the logo was always prominently visible. From there on, we always scored full marks for any photo coverage in any brand evaluation. This format has now become a standard design for any backdrop.

Our long association of over a decade with ITC came to an end when the tobacco bill became a law and ITC stopped all sponsorships.

Another client I enjoyed working with was Hutchinson Max (which first became Orange and then Vodafone) which got the licence to be the operator in Mumbai when cellular telephony was introduced. Our key tasks were getting over the initial response of potential subscribers for the high cost of air time and handsets and highlighting the grid network of Max Touch compared to the mobile network of BPL, our competitor. We accomplished these effectively and became a leader within a few months of the launch.

There were many other clients I handled, but the long relationships with Aditya Birla Group and P&G were especially satisfying.

We expanded from one office in Mumbai to seven offices across the country, with associate arrangements in most tier-2 and tier-3 cities.

Our client roster, steady growth and record of client retention led to a preferred partnership relationship with Ketchum in 2004. Madhukar Kamath, CEO of Mudra, had introduced us to Ketchum, part of Omnicom Inc., which was listed in NYSE. It was then globally the fourth largest PR network. With this partnership, we had access to their clients and latest global practices.

After over seven years of courtship, Ketchum finally formalised the relationship and became Ketchum Sampark in 2011.

We had the soul of a boutique consultancy and always serviced clients at senior levels—our typical client team had more than twenty-five to thirty man-years of experience. Rajan was always hands-on, which was perhaps a key reason for our long retention. With our focus on the credibility and profitability of Sampark, we perhaps declined as many clients as we took.

We were amongst the best performers in the Ketchum system, and in recognition of this, Rajan was invited to become a global partner of Ketchum. In fact, we had personal relationships with all the CEOs of Ketchum in our time, and they made it a point to visit India, which was a sign of the high esteem in which they held this market and our operations.

Rajan and I were present at all annual Ketchum conferences held in Europe and the US. Through these, we heard eminent speakers and attended sessions on best practices with other offices, which kept us abreast of the latest global trends in communications and management.

We developed deep relationships with many of the promoters and CEOs of the companies and groups we worked with. I am especially proud that more than a third of our clients worked with us for a decade or more, and several were with us almost throughout our consultancy life. Over time, we developed a specialisation in crisis communication, and we handled crises for not only our clients but were mandated for special crisis projects by others.

The journey from being an individual practitioner to leading a consultancy with over 150 clients was beyond anything I had ever dreamt of. Reflecting back, I am thankful that I chose PR as a profession, which gave me more than what I expected from life!

On the personal front, besides Sampark, I was also a chairperson of the Mumbai chapter of the FICCI Ladies Organisation (FLO) in 2010–11. It was the year when the then President Barack Obama and his wife visited India and were in Mumbai. As the head of the FLO Mumbai chapter, we were invited and I headed a small delegation to meet their CSR and sustainability head. Our deliberations and my views were subsequently covered in the White House magazine.

Interpretations and Perceptions

When I was working on the ninth PR Congress and later when I joined Consilium Public Relations, PR in India was still in its infancy and was not widely understood. Many of my relatives, friends and people I met had their own interpretations and perceptions about the profession. Everyone knew what advertising was all about, but when it came to PR, their understanding was very foggy—to some, it meant talking smartly and being well-dressed, some confused it with guest relations, i.e., accompanying or entertaining visiting dignitaries, company officials or their wives and family, and to many it was all about wining and dining.

Few understood that PR is an art and science that requires strategic thinking and creativity, with deep understanding of the audiences that an organisation wants to target.

The lack of understanding of PR was not confined to the lay public. In the early days of Sampark, we found that even senior executives of companies were fuzzy about the methodology and efficacy of PR, and we had to market the profession more than ourselves. I distinctly remember that in our early days, our credentials in new pitches were more about:

- What is PR? What can PR do? What PR will not / cannot do?
- How can it help in the marketing mix?
- Can your advertising agency help in your PR programme?
- Do you need specialised help to execute a PR programme?
- How do you measure the success of a PR programme?

The use of PR and its understanding grew dramatically within a few years thanks to the liberalisation wave that swept the country as well as the swift changes in media—the advent of business papers, electronic channels, investigative journalism, etc. The entry of multinationals with their reliance on 360-degree communication also aided the spread and understanding of PR in India.

Initially, PR was mostly about circulating press releases, but in a short time, exclusive stories and compelling content became important largely due to competitive pressures from the entry of new print and electronic media focusing on business.

Most companies realised the efficacy of PR as a practice distinct from advertising and set up their own PR departments or had separate cells as part of their communications team in addition to hiring PR consultancies. At the same time, post 2000, several PR firms came into existence, leading to a talent crunch.

There was a brief halt in the PR profession's growth—once after the financial crisis of 2008 and then again in 2020 due to COVID-19.

While social media, word of mouth and influencers were already making it big in the developed markets, we in India took our time to get there, mostly because internet penetration and adoption caught up in the country much later, with 3G and 4G.

However, India in recent years has caught up with the most sophisticated markets in the practice of PR, just as it has done in very many areas.

Ready for a Major Leap

With the highest growth in GDP among all nations and huge advancement in infrastructure, connectivity and digital penetration to the remotest villages of our country, coupled with the changing face of the media landscape and consumer expectations, PR in India is poised for a great leap.

The opportunities for PR professionals are huge. However, they will increasingly need to focus on engaging and relevant content to reach broader audiences relevant to a brand or service. The use of data analytics to measure PR campaign effectiveness and guide strategy will become increasingly important.

Authentic and compelling storytelling will continue to be a cornerstone of PR, with an increased focus on narratives that resonate on a personal level with the audience. The need for rapid response to crises will intensify with the fast-paced nature of digital communication. Maintaining transparency and building trust will be critical. Emphasis on CSR is increasingly becoming important. Consumers and stakeholders are constantly evaluating this aspect of a company, so PR will have to play a key role in communicating an organisation's CSR efforts and ethical practices. Misleading or deceptive practices will be swiftly called out in the digital age.

The lines between PR, marketing and advertising will continue to blur. Integrated marketing communications (IMC) approaches that combine these will be more effective in delivering cohesive messages. As businesses grow and operate on a global scale, PR campaigns will need to be culturally sensitive and adaptable to different regions and cultures.

Tools like AI, VR and AR technologies will offer innovative ways to engage with the audiences. Engaging employees as corporate and brand ambassadors will become more and more important.

Enhanced awareness and nuanced understanding of sustainability and the environment will be increasingly important, as consumers and stakeholders prioritise eco-friendly practices.

Overall, the future of PR is extremely exciting. Success will hinge on reaching the audiences through appropriate content and the right digital tools, agility in communication, focus on ethical practices and an integrated approach to brand messaging.

PR professionals who adapt to these changes and quickly embrace and leverage new technologies will be well-positioned to succeed in the evolving landscape.

22

N. Sundar Rajan

Co-Founder of Sampark PR (later Ketchum Sampark), currently Chairman, August One Partners LLP

'The beliefs and thoughts of several corporate leaders who were my clients for a long tenure had a profound influence on me and on how Sampark evolved over the next two and a half decades.'

Humble Beginnings

My father worked at ACC (Associated Cement Companies). My mother was originally from South India, but she grew up in Bilaspur, now in Chhattisgarh, as my grandfather worked in the railways. My father grew up in a village, but over time, some of his siblings moved to cities like Chennai and Trichy. Eventually, my father moved to his cousin's house in Mumbai to look for work.

My mother's family was large, with six sisters and three brothers. They all spoke fluent Hindi and English, but my mother didn't know Tamil when she married my father. She had to learn it, and my father was keen that my siblings and I should learn to speak, read and write Tamil.

We studied in a Tamil-medium school until the fourth grade. This school produced very many accomplished individuals, who went on to become prominent figures in industry and private equity. We switched to an English-medium school from fifth to eleventh grade.

While I wasn't very studious, I excelled in general knowledge and kept up with current trends and world events. I eventually graduated with distinction and pursued my interest in finance.

My father passed away when I was just fifteen. So, I had to take on the responsibility of supporting my mother and my younger siblings—my brother was only about ten years old at the time. I ensured that both my sister and brother received proper education and support. My brother eventually became a CA and moved to New York.

While we had an excellent support system through our extended family, those early days were tough. They instilled in me a sense of responsibility, rigour and discipline.

I developed a strong aptitude for finance. I became an active participant in the stock market at the age of fifteen so I could make some extra money while I studied, which also helped me understand market dynamics and their correlation with various economic and financial indicators, thus sharpening my financial knowledge.

I went to RA Poddar College of Commerce and Economics, one of the best commerce colleges of Mumbai in those days. It was located near the home of one of my aunts. I chose that because my aunt was a great cook and I could go there during breaks to have lunch!

Within a few months, I got a job in New India Cooperative Bank, so I moved to morning classes. That's where I met Bela first. Once I graduated, I got placed in ACC, where I worked with their Organisation and Methods (O&M) team for the large part of my tenure and eventually their communications department.

I had accumulated a lot of leaves in ACC and had to exhaust my privilege leaves in order to not let them lapse. In 1987, I took a month's leave to take care of my young twin children. Around that time, a senior journalist contacted me and offered to get me a project to survey investor perception for Essar regarding their shipping company's IPO pricing. The Ruias, the promoters of Essar, thought far ahead of their times and took a thorough and very scientific approach to everything they did, including the marketing of the IPO.

I finished my survey among 200-odd investors and submitted my report and forgot about it. I was paid ₹5000, a princely sum in those days.

Four or five months later, after the IPO was a huge success, I got a call from Essar. I was told that they were happy that the price I had recommended for the IPO was close to the price they used, while another big-bulge MR firm they had hired for a similar survey was way off the mark.

I met the Essar officials, and they offered me an opportunity to join Essar, as they were strengthening the team with people with diverse skills. I could not take up his offer then as it was unthinkable to leave an organisation like ACC, which was a safe haven. My father had worked for over twenty years, and it had nurtured many other family members, including my uncle.

Three years later, in 1989, I met Mr Ravi Ruia (everyone fondly called him Ravi Saab), a director of the group, and he offered me a position in the chairman's secretariat, an opportunity that was difficult to decline.

The seven years that followed at Essar were like doing a PhD for me. I don't think I would have learnt as much at Harvard, Stanford or any Ivy League management school as I did there. I worked very closely with Mr Shashi Ruia and Mr Ravi Ruia, the promoters of Essar, and later with Mr Prashant Ruia. I had a ringside view of a diversified business which was then growing at a phenomenal pace and was exposed to the entire spectrum of the business.

As the executive assistant, I learnt everything: spreadsheets, business, budgeting, management, HR—literally every sphere of business. Over time, I was given additional special responsibility of heading communications and public affairs.

During that time, although I received many job offers, including one that offered me much more compensation than what I was getting at Essar, I turned all of them down. The Ruias and Essar gave me everything I valued: pride, respect and a sense of being truly valued.

However, one gentleman, Mukesh Gupta (Lloyds Steel, Lloyds Finance) was particularly persistent. During one of our meetings, I told him that I wasn't looking for a job at that moment, but as an afterthought I mentioned that I could consider associating with him if he would consider hiring my consultancy, if I were to set up one.

He flatly refused, but six months later, he contacted me again and agreed to my earlier proposition. He was willing to sign me on for a five-year contract with the condition that I dedicate a certain number of hours to his businesses.

By that time, I knew many journalists who had become dear friends. Back then, our relationships were very genuine and personal. These friendships extended beyond business; some of them were part of our personal lives. When I consulted them about my career move, they encouraged me to go for it. While the thought of becoming an entrepreneur was exhilarating, I faced a dilemma. My worry was that if I took up the Lloyds offer, I would be a one-client consultancy, which was in some ways employment in another garb, and I expressed my inhibitions to Mr Mukesh Gupta. It was indeed magnanimous of Mr Gupta to understand me and my predicament. In the span of a few weeks, he had spoken to his business associates and secured me three additional clients with long-term retainers and sign-on fees.

However, leaving Essar was difficult. There were several unfinished projects that I had taken up and thought it was inappropriate to leave without completing them.

It took me over a year to finally separate and join Bela, who was already running Sampark with few clients on retainer and several clients working with her on a project basis for their PR requirements. On 1 August 1994, we started out as a private limited company in a small cubicle in Nariman Point with five long-term retainers and several project clients, and never looked back.

Lloyds, ABB, SKF Bearings, Welspun, Weizmann and Videocon were among our first big clients, but our big break came when Sampark signed up with Hutchinson Max when cellular telephony came to India. Another break was when we signed on DSP Merrill Lynch.

The beliefs and thoughts of several corporate leaders who were my clients for a long tenure had a profound influence on me and on how Sampark evolved over the next two-and-a-half decades. I shall be eternally grateful to them for not only how I ran the business, but also how I developed as an individual. Among the many clients I admired and learnt from, the following three lessons stand out.

DSP had just entered into a joint venture with the then big-bulge investment bank Merrill Lynch for an asset management company. Hemendra Kothari, the then chairman of DSP Merrill Lynch, India and chairman of DSP Group, who has been father figure to us and stayed with us throughout our consultancy life, taught me transparency, honesty and adherence to governance. The most important lesson from him was that being ethical is the only way to get the trust and respect of your clients and have long-term relationships with them.

The favourite maxim of Rajiv Bajaj, MD of Bajaj Auto, another client who worked with us till the end, was 'Less is more', and he practised this across all Bajaj Auto initiatives. So at Sampark, we focused on the most profitable segments like finance, corporate, technology and crisis and were underweight in many other sectors.

Aditya Puri, the then MD of HDFC Bank, with which Sampark had a relationship of over fifteen years, wanted to be the most profitable and respected bank not necessarily the biggest bank, and we tried to apply this to Sampark all the time.

Media Disruptions and Integrated Strategies

It was early days for PR back when we started our firm. I had to explain to potential clients, including CEOs and CFOs, what PR was and what it could do to a brand and how it was different from advertising.

We were blessed that when we started in the late 1990s and early 2000s, many changes occurred in the business and marketing landscape of India, which gave a fillip to services: a wave of liberalisation was sweeping the country, which opened up many new areas like cellular telephony, several segments in financial services like private sector banking, investment banking, private equity and venture capital, mutual funds and then insurance, etc. We had the opportunity to work with leaders in these new segments, which had opened up in addition to the traditional areas.

Many large multinational consumer and industrial brands made a beeline for India. Just to illustrate, when ITC was launching B&H and 555, BAT, the parent of ITC at that time, wanted a PR firm to handle the launch. We were fortunate to be tasked with this. There on, we got the opportunity to manage ITC's entire portfolio of brands and sponsorships. Over time, several Indian corporates also started discovering the efficacy of PR and adopted it in their marketing mix. With all these came newer practices, including a preference to hire an external consultancy to supplement in-house staff.

Perhaps the one defining change was the explosive growth of media and its fractionalisation. That made the PR need and delivery both challenging and exhilarating. It was no longer about a newspaper story or a TV channel—it was all about ways to influence opinion that all types of traditional and new media had opened up and yet remained focused on the message.

The advent of investigative journalism, twenty-four-hour news channels and wire services, entry of more business publications, more business pages in general media, investor and consumer activism, Indian corporate's desire to enhance shareholder value and changing regulatory framework and disclosure norms—all of these contributed at different points to making crisis communication a more defined and specialised practice within the ambit of PR. Today, a large corporate cannot afford to wait for a crisis to occur to learn how to handle one. We found ourselves more and more involved in assignments to prepare businesses to handle crises *before* they occurred.

By 2011–12, the more developed markets had moved away from traditional PR into digital, influencer, word of mouth, etc. In fact, when I walked into the Ketchum global meets in the past, I would feel like a stranger to many of the discussions, as did some of my colleagues from the Asian markets. We took time to get there, mostly because internet penetration and adoption caught up in India much later.

One big difference I saw in the west was the quality of talent. In the developed markets, firms were able to attract the best talent, while in India, PR remained in some ways a cheaper alternative to expensive advertising campaigns. And consequently, we remained relatively underpaid by clients.

Continuous training is another aspect that needs more attention. I found that upskilling people not only benefits clients but also keeps the morale and motivation of employees high over the long term. The advertising agencies scored higher on this count.

Proliferation of social media in the last decade and a half only further accentuated the need for communications in the continual success of people and brands. Today, most good firms have specialised cells with people who are trained and experienced. They are familiar with regulatory frameworks and completely understand the pulse of their constituents.

Adapting to Rapid Changes and Emerging Opportunities

India is on the cusp of a huge leap over the next many years, which will bring immense opportunities to services, including the PR business and PR professionals. India is on track to become the world's third largest economy by 2027, surpassing Japan and Germany, and will have the third largest stock market by 2030 thanks to global trends and key investments the country has made in technology and energy.

India is also poised to become the factory to the world aided by the China+ factor. Multinationals are now buoyant about the prospects of investing in India. Almost every Fortune 500 company that missed joining the bandwagon has announced their India plans or are currently evaluating their India entry.

India's overall consumption could more than double as income consumption and distribution in the country expands. Folks in rural areas will help increase the per capita income. Smartphone penetration is currently at 80 per cent of the population, which presents a huge canvas to communicators.

All of India's 6,00,000-plus villages now have access to electricity, due to recent upgrades to transmission and distribution. Digital payments such as the unified payments interface (UPI), formalisation of credit (with account aggregator networks), plugging revenue leakages, introduction of GST, huge investments in infrastructure including roads, railways and airports—all are measures taken over the last decade that have aided India's competitiveness.

Banking penetration has gone up. Together with the demographic dividend, these developments foretell huge opportunities for Indians. So, the future for Indian industry is bright and for employees brighter, especially in a service sector like PR, aided by newer tools like AI, VR and AR.

Of course, there will be challenges like increased activism, investor scrutiny, global norms, climate change-related emission norms, more stringent norms for products and services, reaching out to the fringe consumer, etc. But these very challenges will create a huge demand for communication and PR services, and the sector is expected to boom and reward those who adapt quickly to the changing times and needs in the coming years.

The consolidation of current MNCs and the entry of new ones, the culture of entrepreneurship and the start-up boom will open up new avenues for trained and competent Indian PR professionals, not only in India but also in all corners of the world.

Several communications personnel have started moving to global positions in multinationals in the last few years. This will only increase in the future. I believe the next many years will bring exciting potential to the PR professionals in India. After all, I believe Indians are among the smartest brains in the world.

23

Prema Sagar

Founder of Genesis PR, currently Chairperson Emeritus, Burson Group India

'My foray into PR was also a mix of my will to always push my boundaries and a healthy dose of luck!'

The Fauji Kid Who Built a PR Enterprise

My childhood was idyllic. I am from a Fauji family. My father was an officer in the Indian Air Force (he later rose to be an air marshal), and my childhood was spent at the various Air Force stations at which he was posted. My brother and I were raised in an environment where integrity and values were more important than anything else. My father demonstrated throughout his life by standing his ground on matters of principle. He did so many a time at great cost to himself, including denial and deferral of hard-earned recognition and rewards.

My mother left Switzerland, all by herself, boarding a ship to come to India to be with my father. She had her own set of values that she ensured were rooted deeply in us—values of orderliness, discipline, compassion, kindness and community service. I was a bit of a rebel and would get into confrontations with my father. While my brother would retreat into his corner, with his guitar and chess, I would get into all kinds of trouble! My teachers and parents coped with it as best as they could. For instance, at the Sacred Heart Girls' High School and at the Good Shepherd Convent in Bangalore, they would entrust me with responsibilities and that kept me out of trouble!

When I completed tenth grade, my father was posted in Nagpur, where I studied at Hislop College for a year. The college and the city held no challenge for me, and I was very keen to escape them both to study at Shri Ram College of Commerce (SRCC) in New Delhi. I applied, got on the merit list and found a room in a women's hostel. It was everything I had hoped for at first. Soon, though, I realised that small town or big, the world always had opinions on how women should live their lives. I, on the other hand, wanted to live life on my terms. So, I soon left SRCC as well.

After leaving college, I joined a secretarial course at YMCA. As I finished the course, my cousin, who worked as a receptionist at the law firm Sagar & Co. left her job to get married. I joined the firm as her replacement. That was a huge learning experience for me. I volunteered to do more than my job description and understood the intricacies of how an organisation works. This is where I also met my husband, Jyoti. In 1976, against all odds and all sorts of objections, we got married. I went on to do a couple of other secretarial jobs, till the time I had my first child—our son Rahul. Once he was a couple of years old, I realised I needed to get back to work and wanted to set up my own business. My brother, who was so far managing a tea garden in the east, decided to join me too. This was a big and unprecedented step for us. We scraped the bottom of the barrel, so to say, and with a bank-financed printing machine, set up Genesis Printers in 1981. My father was aghast. He said that we were not a business family, after all. I told him that we could always make a beginning, and that is how the name 'Genesis' came about! I managed the marketing and accounts, while my brother managed the operations.

Like everything in my life, my foray into PR was also a mix of my will to always push my boundaries and a healthy dose of luck! In 1984, I started publishing a magazine called *Genesis – The City Guide*—this was a typical guide for tourists and was placed in hotel rooms. During this time, I came into contact with several hotels in Delhi. One of these was The Park Hotel, owned by the Apeejay Surrendra Group. Priya Paul, who at a young age had taken over the management of the group following the tragic and untimely death of her father, was looking at building the reputation of the hotel and increasing the footfall. She asked me to help her in that task. They did not have any significant advertising budget and one had to think of a different way of spreading the word.

During a break in Kasauli, I was reading Mark McCormack's book *On Communicating*. That gave me an idea, which I presented to Priya. Thus was born 'Going Public at the Park', a monthly event, where The Park would invite a high-profile person to come as a speaker. People could come to the hotel to listen and to interact with the speaker. In the process, the attendees would experience the facilities at and hospitality of The Park. The invitees also included people from the media. Based on the success of this concept, we created 'Theatre at the Park', 'Cinema at the Park' and 'Christmas at the Park'. I didn't know it then, but what we had done was PR!

The second serendipitous event was running into Cecil Dewars, the Delhi office head of Ogilvy PR, in The Park

Hotel lobby. He gave me a book by a very well-respected PR guru, Frank Jefkins. The book, quite literally, changed my life. I knew then that I wanted to learn from him. So, I wrote to him and enrolled in a course he ran in London. This was my formal introduction to the world of PR.

When I came back from London after completing the course, I had only one objective—to build India's most professional PR firm. And so, in November 1992, Genesis PR was born. It was a fortuitous time. India's economy had opened up in July 1991. There was an influx of companies from all over the world, and they brought with them global standards and expectations in everything, including PR. Our Indian companies, many of whom were eager to collaborate with these multinationals, were poised to gain much from incorporating PR into their marketing and functional mix. They had a long way to go, though. I knew that we needed to do PR for PR. And so, along with seeding and growing my own business, I set about collaborating with the few practitioners we had back then to create the foundation of a profession. Former editor of *The Financial Express* Y.C. Halan also encouraged me to write about issues relating to PR and gave us the opportunity to come across as thought leaders.

Soon after I set up shop, a few people came into my life, giving me just the right nudges to help me realise my dream. Two of them, Geeta Singh and Archana Jain, and soon after, Nandita Lakshmanan. There were four of us servicing three clients—Thai Airways, Travel House and of course, The Park Hotels, which is a relationship that continues even now, more than three decades later! Another person I remember fondly is Kavin Sethi, then the PR manager at Lufthansa. We would constantly be locking horns with each other on issues and nuances of PR. Kavin moved to Genesis, but most unfortunately, we lost him to cancer after a couple of years.

Tarun Das, the legendary secretary general of the Confederation of Indian Industry (CII), was another strong influence in my life. He gave us the unique opportunity to manage the PR for the Indo-British Partnership Initiative (IBPI), a high-profile event in Mumbai, where the events on board the Royal Yacht were the highlight. That gave us the launchpad to enter the big league.

There are a few ways we have always stood apart from everyone else in the business. First, our conviction, from the beginning, that we will not seek business growth at the cost of integrity and ethics. We stand by that even today. The value system at our firm has been a constant.

Second, never giving in to the status quo. We have always endeavoured to think ahead of client needs. We kept investing aggressively in the business to build capability, expand our service offerings and create differentiators that would help us support our clients with their evolving needs.

These included differentiated services such as public affairs, content and, later, digital, influencer marketing, data analytics. More recently, we have added corporate social purpose, employee advocacy and executive visibility. We were also the first to introduce practice areas: industries, services, brands, sports and entertainment, IT and telecom, healthcare and others.

Technology was to be our differentiator from the get-go. Back when we started, many of our clients didn't have a computer for every employee, but we ensured that there was one on each desk. Over the years, we continued to leverage technology for the growth of our people, our clients and, ultimately, our firm. And now, as part of Burson and WPP, we are again at the leading edge of technology innovation in the profession, building solutions that harness AI and other emerging technologies to build reputation capital.

Third, but perhaps the most crucial, was investing in the growth of talent in the profession and our firm. Our flagship Associate Learning Programme turns twenty this year, and we have continued to add and enhance the ambit of our School of Learning. We are who we are because of our people, and contributing to their growth is a priority. And not just people in our firm—we have also nurtured emerging talent by visiting campuses and sharing our knowledge with them. That is why people who have worked with us don't just think of us as an employer but as an institution.

Over the years, we have taken several leaps. In 2005, we were acquired by Burson-Marsteller, which also brought us into the fold of WPP. In 2018, WPP merged B-M with Cohn & Wolfe to create BCW. In 2024, BCW and H&K Strategies merged to create Burson. Through all of this, we have managed to retain the name Genesis, as we are known today as Burson Genesis. This is a huge testament to the legacy we have built in these thirty-one years.

Since our journey began when the PR discipline was nascent, we had to literally pave the path before us. That happened on the back of some seminal work in two areas—helping build new categories and expanding the definition of PR by developing new expertise.

The second area was to build new categories. Over the years, we have helped lay the foundation for several industry categories. For the travel, tourism and aviation industry, for instance, we were there right from the beginning—our first client, as I said, was The Park Hotels, and we followed that up by signing on Lufthansa and Travel House. We also partnered with InterGlobe when the first IndiGo flight took off, and we continue to work with them. We continued to add clients in the sector, including several hotels, airlines and even the tourism boards of several countries.

Another major industry we helped was telecom, where we have supported hardware, network, as well as service provider clients. We were instrumental in setting up the Indian Cellular Association, have had several handset companies as clients and supported Vodafone through its growth journey till the landmark merger with Idea to form Vi.

Supporting the entertainment and sports verticals are our other major achievements.

Through our work, we expanded the definition of PR. As one of the first movers in the industry, we had to build the PR practice and what it comprises along the way.

Back in 1996, we sowed the seeds of public affairs. There was an influx of multinationals after liberalisation, and many were in areas unfamiliar to policymakers, and we saw the opportunity to bridge the gap. As time went on, the policy and regulatory environment grew more and more complex, and our PA practice evolved to partner with our clients every step of the way. Today, the practice provides invaluable counsel for companies to navigate the uncertain geopolitical and dynamic policy environment.

We also laid the foundations of crisis communication. Early in the day, I met Tapan Mitra, the then MD of the aluminium major Indal, who said he didn't feel the need for crisis preparedness. However, soon there was an issue in one of their factories and he reached out to me. We used that opportunity to set up a crisis management framework for them. This base work helped us when there was a hostile takeover bid on the company. We moved with bag and baggage to Mumbai, where we sat alongside lawyers and bankers to help them tackle it. This wasn't something we understood, but once again, we set out to understand the issue and then made Tapan visit several media offices to meet the editor, to explain his point of view, and saw the narrative change from negative to positive. These early steps and lessons in crisis management are something we still live by. In 2005, we were standing shoulder-to-shoulder with Pepsi during the pesticide crisis. Most recently, we helped manage the existential crisis that Maggi Noodles faced.

Over and over, we anticipated the 'what next' for clients and kept reshaping the industry with new service lines, such as the first of its kind Live! Newsroom; providing data-driven intelligence for promoting, protecting and measuring reputation; Canvas for films and design; Alphabet for content and editorial services; and Digital. We also created a dedicated offering for startups called Step Up, a Corporate Social Purpose (CSP+) division for helping companies lead with purpose, and of course, now AI.

From Fax Machine to Digital Media

To understand how PR has evolved in the last two decades, especially in India, you must consider how India in general and India Inc. in particular has evolved. As I mentioned, when I started Genesis PR, the Indian economy was just opening its doors to the world. Liberalisation paved the way for global companies to come here—India was a vast untapped market. To connect with the audience, they relied on both advertising and PR. But it was a different world. Back then, fax machines whirred with press releases, press conferences were the Holy Grail of media outreach and building relationships with journalists meant long lunches. As a young entrepreneur who dared to dream of a different kind of PR firm, this transactional approach never sat right with me. I wanted PR to not just be about securing placements but about building trust, fostering genuine connections and shaping narratives that resonated with a purpose.

Enter the internet revolution. The internet's biggest disruption was that information flow went from being one-way to two-way. The rise of social media further democratised communication, empowering people to become both consumers and content creators. PR professionals, used to the controlled environment of press briefings, had to learn to navigate the rapids of this real-time, two-way conversation change.

This shift demanded a new skill set. While still important, media relations became just one part of what we did. Content marketing, crisis communication expertise and a deep understanding of digital analytics became essential. In short, PR was not just about media and businesses. It became the only marketing discipline that could touch all the stakeholders of an organisation. Therefore, our understanding of all these stakeholders, as well as the best way to connect with them, had to be enhanced.

The internet and social media also expanded our horizons. Indian consumers, increasingly exposed to global trends, began to demand more from brands. They craved authenticity, transparency and a sense of shared purpose. This shift in consumer behaviour fundamentally changed the way we approached PR. The focus shifted from simply promoting products to building genuine connections with consumers based on shared values. Brands had to tell their stories with a human touch, demonstrate a commitment to social responsibility and actively engage in conversations on issues that mattered to their audience.

The past four years have seen disruption on steroids. How we think, feel, behave and therefore communicate has fundamentally changed. It is a post-truth world, and therefore, reputation is not just built on truth and fact but also on belief. As custodians of our clients' reputations, our work is cut out for us.

Embracing Technology with AI and VR Innovations

Let me start by stating the obvious: data analytics and technologies like AI and AR / VR have transformed PR and communications. AI tools are streamlining workflows and analysing vast amounts of data to identify trends and predict audience behaviour. Generative AI has made creative content sharper, better and faster. Data analytics empower us to measure the impact of our efforts with unprecedented precision. We can now go beyond vanity metrics and demonstrate our PR activities' true ROI.

However, technology is just one instrument in the PR orchestra. While AI excels at crunching numbers and identifying patterns, it lacks the emotional intelligence fundamental to effective communication. I think PR is, at its core, a human endeavour. The ability to understand context, navigate nuance and connect with people at an emotional level—these are skills that AI simply cannot replicate. I am returning to my first brush with PR at The Park Hotel. No amount of AI could have given people the experiences that events like 'Going Public at the Park' and 'Theatre at the Park' gave. And it is this experience that converted into footfalls and increased occupancy at the hotel.

Similarly, the power to navigate a crisis with grace lies in human judgement. AI can analyse historical data on similar situations, but it cannot anticipate the nuances of a specific situation or the emotional undercurrents at play. A seasoned PR professional, with their understanding of the media landscape—including digital media—and their ability to think strategically under pressure, can guide a company through a crisis with its reputation intact.

The fundamentals of storytelling also remain timeless. Crafting a compelling narrative that resonates with an audience requires human creativity. AI may be able to generate text, but it cannot write a post that tugs at the heartstrings.

The future of PR lies in the marriage of human and technological expertise. AI and data will continue to streamline processes and provide valuable insights, but the human element—the storyteller, the strategist, the empathetic communicator—will always be irreplaceable. The future PR professional will be a hybrid—someone who can leverage the power of technology while staying grounded in the core principles of reputation management.

It is important to embrace technology with open arms, harness these new tools and hone our data literacy. But we can never forget the power of human connection—the ability to understand, empathise and build trust. This, combined with the power of technology, will be the winning formula for PR success in the years to come.

24

Rishi Seth

Founding Partner of Six Degrees, currently Investor and Partner, The PRactice

'As communicators, our role is to bridge connections between organisations, individuals and their audiences. Whether it's conveying a brand's message or facilitating interactions between people with shared interests, our aim is to facilitate these connections.'

Entrepreneurship Ran in the Family

I was born and raised in Delhi as part of a joint family involved in the automobile trade. With my father, uncle and grandfather deeply involved in the industry, it seemed natural for me to follow suit. After completing my schooling at DPS, Mathura Road, and college at Delhi University, I found myself fortunate to pursue an MBA in marketing.

I was eager to join my father's business, but my mother said, 'You've earned an MBA, so perhaps you should consider not joining your father's business.' And I said, 'No, it's comfortable. I'd just be sitting in a shop, handling transactions. It's a good life, being the boss from day one.' However, she insisted, encouraging me to give it a two-year trial period. She assured me that if I wished to return to the family business after two years, the option would still be there. Surprisingly, after two years, I did contemplate joining my father's business while working with Video on Wheels, earning a salary of around ₹10,000. Yet, when I requested the same amount from my father, he declined. That refusal made me reconsider my decision, ultimately leading me to abstain from joining the family business.

My entry into the professional world began with rural marketing in 1995, a time when the internet had yet to proliferate and traditional media held sway in rural areas. Working with Video on Wheels, I travelled extensively, promoting products and engaging customers across villages. However, despite the interesting work, I soon realised the limited growth prospects in the company. This prompted me to seek new opportunities, leading me to Perfect Relations, where I spent my formative years, despite having minimal exposure to PR prior to my MBA studies.

I spent five years at Perfect Relations, initially joining as an account executive and eventually rising to the position of team leader. Following that, I transitioned to Genesis, where I unexpectedly found myself leading the technology practice in Delhi. Although it wasn't a planned move, my understanding of technology garnered recognition, and I was entrusted with numerous tech-related mandates, drawing from my previous experience at Perfect Relations. After my tenure at Genesis, lasting nearly a year, I moved on to Text100 (now known as Archetype). There, I spent almost a decade, beginning as an account director and ultimately leaving as country manager.

I began by overseeing a substantial team that handled clients such as Cisco, NASSCOM and British Telecom. Subsequently, I was promoted to branch head, and then I advanced further in my role. Those nine and a half years at Text100 were truly remarkable. The business grew rapidly, establishing a solid reputation in the market. Despite the success, I found myself pondering what to pursue next. That's when Zacharia James (Zach) and I, who had mostly aligned our careers, sat down over drinks to brainstorm. Zach had already ventured into a content company called Alphabet Consulting, having left a year and a half or so earlier. Meanwhile, I contemplated leaving Text100 and exploring new avenues.

Zach and I deliberated on a few ideas, one of which involved blending our experiences from working at Indian-founded firms like Dilip and Bobby's Perfect Relations and Prema's Genesis with our multinational exposure from Text100. We aimed to create a unique consultancy structure, combining the best elements of both worlds. It was a test of our capabilities and learnings, culminating in the birth of Six Degrees. This marked yet another phase of invaluable learning experiences for us.

Why Six Degrees? The concept of six degrees of separation intrigued us. It suggests that everyone in the world is connected by just six interpersonal links. Initially a theory in sociology, it's now influenced by the internet and social media, possibly reducing the degree of separation to four or three. We found inspiration in this idea because as communicators, our role is to bridge connections between organisations and individuals and their audiences. Whether it's conveying a brand's message or facilitating interactions between people with shared interests, our aim is to facilitate these connections. Hence, the name Six Degrees. Like many of our creative concepts, this one also emerged during casual discussions over drinks. Six Degrees exceeded our expectations, growing rapidly and making a significant impact.

Our initial client was Hughes Communications, a satellite broadband company with whom we had worked previously. They transitioned from being a Text100 client. Following that, we secured EMC in Bangalore, albeit not initially for their primary mandate. Instead, we undertook a project to establish the GCC in Bangalore, which proved highly successful. Consequently, we secured the entire EMC mandate, and then Bird Group. We then won landmark clients like IKEA, PepsiCo, Google, Volkswagen and many more.

Initially, we focused heavily on technology because of our network's tech-centric nature over the past decade. However, we later diversified into other sectors such as consumer goods, automotive and, to a lesser extent, banking and fintech. Recognising market disruptions, particularly in social and digital realms, Zach and I sought international partnerships for technological insights and social media expertise, given the advanced markets in the US and UK. After evaluating numerous firms, we found a fitting partner in Cohn & Wolfe. (Cohn & Wolfe later went on to merge with Burson Marsteller as BCW and is now rebranded as Burson.)

The first three or four people who joined us were almost as entrepreneurial as Zach and me. They took a leap of faith with Six Degrees and came to us with strong pedigree and a zest to try something new. Amongst the first few employees were Supriya Gupta, Anika Gupta, Vilsha Kapoor and Pooja Poddar. None of them had any connection with us through Text100. One of the most satisfying outcomes of founding Six Degrees is having worked with a wonderful band of communications professionals taking the profession forward.

We aimed to foster a robust culture and instil passion within our team, which contributed to minimal turnover at the senior- and mid-level. While junior staff turnover occurred due to compensation factors, our stability among mid- to senior-level personnel, some of whom remained until the end of Zach and my tenure, was pivotal to our success. This ensured continuity and belief in Six Degrees, facilitating our business growth.

The Two Decades of Liberalisation and Media Growth

The PR consulting business in India was founded in the early 1990s by a few path-breaking founders. PR in its infancy was sometimes seen as a protocol and guest relations function with a focus largely on being a media coverage factory. During the next two decades, it went through a phase, where liberalisation and the growth of the media in a developing economy like India gave the PR sector a lot of opportunity. It provided a wide array of services for corporates, political parties and celebrities to understand the organic media space and the benefits it can provide.

The drive towards professionalism in corporates, both multinational and domestic, led to consulting firms thriving in India. Political parties and celebrities soon saw the benefits of expert advice and, today, some of the smartest communications teams are servicing political parties, leaders and celebrities from all spheres of society. Movie actors and sports champions attract some of the best talent in the profession.

From a service portfolio and expertise perspective, the scope of services has expanded dramatically, and I would say that the PR professional today has a more important role than even the traditional brand and creative leaders. The essential element that has tilted the balance in their favour is the advent of social media and two-way communication as opposed to the one-way communication of the past. Today, you cannot expect to build a brand just by bombarding them with an aggressive media campaign—it takes much more!

A brand / company / personality gets direct feedback and comments from their stakeholders. This could relate to the product or the service that they are offering or a corporate decision, where shareholders will participate in a conversation with the company on public platforms. Before social media, a sense of controlling the narrative existed due to the use of managed content to drive the narrative—any counter to this did not get a voice. Today, you have many ways to check inaccurate or inauthentic information, and the communicator has to be much more transparent to gain the audience's trust. Money and resources are still used and misused to drive online narratives, but it keeps getting harder and more expensive.

I can correlate this with a political campaign experience, since it is the flavour of the season. During the late 1990s, I got the opportunity to work for the Congress (I) party in the national elections. For the daily briefing, a communications committee from the party would go over the agenda of news that had appeared, issues raised and then decide on the core narrative for the day. This would be translated into a media note, and a briefing would happen from the party every day.

Today, as I follow political parties, the communication velocity, content and messaging are so different and intense. Teams are so much more agile, with so many more analytic and creative resources at hand to address any opportunity or clarify any misinformation very quickly. I can imagine a core group managing communications being in war rooms and in touch through various collaborative groups, identifying, strategising, creating and responding through a slew of mediums on a real-time basis.

The communications function has come a long way in the last twenty years and is today considered as an important profession for any entity or individual who intends to engage stakeholders. It is also a growing profession, with lots of successful consulting firms and large corporate communications teams. The sector has brought in a decent amount of investment into the country, considering the acquisitions being made. Finally, it provides our young generation a prosperous and stimulating career opportunity.

The Impact of Technology on Business

PR is going through a transformation as a profession due to the advancements in technology and how it impacts every sphere of business. The fact that the medium for communications will be dominated by digital is a no-brainer, but this does not mean that the importance of key influencers will reduce. It will shift from media houses being the primary source of information to subject matter experts and online content aggregators also being equal participants.

In terms of focus areas, I would imagine that depending on the kind of primary role that the organisation needs, a PR person might seem to be a product marketing specialist in one company, a reputation counsellor in another or part of the talent and people team. We are therefore seeing specialists come out in horizontal service lines also.

Organic media content will no longer define the scope of a PR professional's intervention. The fraternity will take the lead on all four aspects of content—PESO (paid, earned, shared and owned)—and will use all mediums possible to amplify the communication. In fact, this is already well underway—just that the capabilities and resources in building these services will significantly go up in the next few years. This also means that the next few years are a time of investment for the profession, which might also lead to some consolidation.

Talent requirement for the PR profession will also undergo a sea change. The profession will need a diverse talent base of people, including creative talent, visual and design content experts, data and analytic scientists, prompt engineers and many more.

A PR professional will have information, data, insights and creative tools driven by technology, which were never available to the profession before. This will add the element of science / data / analytics to the art of PR. A massive upskill in talent is on the anvil, and I think the businesses will compete with many other sectors for people and not just from communication schools.

Newer models of commercial engagement will also emerge in the PR business. We are already seeing performance-based variable fees being made part of contracts. Consequently, the fixed fee component might reduce as part of the total compensation. Given the nature of work, engagement will be more specific with clear outcome metrics. This means the measurement and ROI evaluation frameworks will also get revalidated.

Acknowledgements

From Sarika Chavan

I WANT TO THANK MY FATHER, THE LATE ANIL SALIAN, FOR everything he has done for me—his guidance, love and unwavering support has shaped my journey in ways I cannot fully express. To my mother, Laxmi Salian, for always believing in me and standing by my side, even in moments of doubt. My deepest gratitude to my beautiful daughters, Sia and Saisha, for their patience and understanding as they endured my tantrums throughout this process. And, to my husband, Sachin—thank you for being my rock, my constant source of strength and encouragement.

I have had the immense pleasure of co-editing this book with Amith Prabhu, a mentor and a friend whose belief in me has pushed me to achieve more than I ever thought possible. His constant reminder to never underestimate my potential has been a driving force behind this project—thank you, Amith, for your guidance, support and faith in me.

A special thank you to Westland—Karthika, Amrita, Aurodeep and the rest of the team—for believing in the concept of this book and helping us bring it to life. Their support was instrumental in curating this masterpiece of twenty-four gem-like stories, each unique, each told from the heart.

From Amith Prabhu

I remain grateful to my parents—Sukhdeep and the late Ethel Prabhu—for pushing me to read and write. To my wife Suchetha and daughter Swara, who runs the show and makes me run, respectively. To my partners at work—Roshan Alexander, Anubhuti Mathur and Ameeta Vadhera: you are the wind beneath my wings.

A special thanks to fellow Mangalorean Sarika Chavan, who believed in this idea with her eyes closed and made this happen. Ninety per cent of the heavy lifting was done by her in less than 100 days. She can write a book a year if she chooses to. Some dreams can come true.

Thanks to Geo George—our designer friend who created the logo for this project. Grateful to Moksh Juneja—our friend in digital marketing who helped build the website with his team.

The PR Pioneers

(arranged in alphabetical order by second name)

Sunil Agarwal

Atul Ahluwalia

Madan Bahal (right)
with Rajesh Chaturvedi

Manisha Chaudhary

Kunal Kishore Sinha

Dilip Cherian

Rajiv Desai

Sunil Gautam

Aman Gupta

Shivani Gupta

Vineet Handa

Archana Jain

Ashish Jalan

Zacharia James

Samir Kale

Bobby Kewalramani

Nikhil Khanna

Nandita Lakshmanan

Gaurav Patra

Bela Rajan

Roger Pereira

N. Sundar Rajan

Prema Sagar

Rishi Seth

LIGHT A SPARK